I’m Not Talking Fast, You’re Just Listening Slow
(The measure of a man)

I'm Not Talking Fast, You're Just Listening Slow
(The measure of a man)

SPENCER L. BARNETT

Photo by Ashley M. Barnett

Editing by Kim Luong and crgreen4editing@gmail.com

Cover: Joanna Dame and Marcus Kiser

Published by Spencer Lee Barnett\2WorldsEntertainment

Semi-Autobiography

Some names, times, and events have been changed.

ISBN: 978-0-615-32506-4

Printed in the United States of America

Acknowledgements

Thank you, my Lord and Savior, for my life. You are the provider of my all. I ask that You bless this project, that it may help save a life or inspire someone to do better. Thank you, my Lord, for giving me a second chance at this thing called Life. I will do my best to uplift Your Name and live a prosperous life in Jesus name. Amen.

I would like to thank my family which has been very patient and understanding throughout the entire process of me putting my life on paper: Your love and support for me was endless and constantly pushed me to continue telling my story, even when I veered off course. It did not go unnoticed. I love you all dearly: Gloria l. Barnett, Ashley Barnett, Madison Barnett, Sydney Barnett, Mercedes Barnett

To my lovely mother, Annie Marie, who devoted all of her love, determination and drive to provide the best she could, for not giving up on us even when we didn't always make good decisions: Thank you for protecting and supporting us to the best of your ability. I love you.

To my father, Henry: You weren't always the best father figure back then, but you are the father I need right now-- I love you.

To my brother, Marvin, and his wife, Tonya Barnett: Thank you guys for your love and knowing you both will always have my back is greatly appreciated.

To my little sister, Shakeena Barnett, who I love with all my heart: Thank you for allowing me to be your big brother--it's an honor. To my brother-in-law, Quinell Robinson: I know you will take good care of her.

To my niece, Otia, and my nephew, Johnny: Stop arguing so much--LOL. I love you both.

Thanks, also to the troops: Jeffery, Miles, Landon, Jasmine, Briana.

To my uncles--James, Kenny, Tony, Terry Morrison, Ben, and Bobby Seabrooks: Thanks for all your support.

To the world's best aunties: Charlie, Peaches, Carolyn, Patricia, and my baby, Linda: Thank you for being who you are and playing a crucial role in my life.

Dedication

Dedicated to the memory of:
Charles Jackson and Maybelle Jackson

To Charles Jackson, my cousin and my friend:

I miss you and always wonder what your life would've been like today. We didn't get to spend much time together, but I thank God for the time He gave us together growing up on Siegle Avenue. I love you.

To Maybelle Jackson, the very best grandmother ever:

I miss you so much and I clearly remember the times you would sit me down and talk to me about being a man. I still wink at others, like we would always do. I know you see me wink at you every night. I have never told a soul what you told me, but I'm doing it now, Ma, I'm doing it! I love you.

I'M NOT TALKING FAST, YOU'RE JUST LISTENING SLOW
(The measure of a man)

SPENCER L. BARNETT

Foreword

You are about to embark on a pleasant and encouraging journey. The information and ideas shared in this book can lay the groundwork for change that you are seeking to make in your life.

This book is written in Basic English and filled with the writer's emotions; it is filled with real life experiences which you may identify with.

The stories of encounters are examples of everyday challenges that life may present. What is unique and refreshing is the author's perspective and reactions, which you will find to be very inspiring and uplifting. To each of our lives there is purpose, begin to discover your purpose with reading the pages that follow.

Romans: Eight and Twenty-Eight

Oscar Agurs

Preface

The story of my life was being written in my head for years. Not until I realized that my story could help someone else did I decide to share my life experiences with others. I hope that it will make a difference in someone's life.

It all started when I was giving motivational speeches in the Think Smart Program. In this program I went to schools and talked to young kids about my life experiences, the bad decisions I made, and how they affected me and all that was around me.

I loved giving the speeches--it made me feel like I was giving back to the community.

Motivated, by the impact I had on the kids, I posted my notes on a few websites about my life's experiences, hoping to inspire others with my words of encouragement. I received positive feedback from people who looked forward to reading my posts to inspire them to get through the day. I dedicated myself to supporting others who needed to boost their self esteem and also to increase their confidence.

Many of the readers appreciated and thanked me for taking the time to post optimistic statements. They needed to hear words of encouragement. One lady even told me she had not ventured out in the sun until I touched her with my words. She stepped out for the first time, after years of being trapped inside her house due to her traumatic experiences.

I was elated to hear that I had helped someone—I wanted to continue to serve God with what He had instilled in me. I decided to write down my thoughts and express my feelings as well as tell about my life experiences.

People often ask me how I stay positive and happy all the time. I tell them, "Everything after waking up is a bonus. God has given me a second chance at this thing called Life. I don't take life for granted because I know I am blessed. In order for people to understand the man I am today, they need to know who I was, and where I came from. I have seen and experienced things in my life that many people could not imagine. A lot of the things people can identify with.

Often people think things are so bad for themselves, not realizing that others are experiencing worse things. I wrote this book to give people hope and the understanding of how things may start one way, but if you keep God in your life, things can get better.

This book is not written to glorify criminal activities or to blame anyone for things that happened in the past. This is about my journey to becoming a man. I hope the book, inspires you and gives you hope and makes you realize not to take things in life for granted.

This book is to show people that I believed in my God-given abilities and I stepped out on faith to discover the true measure of a man. I hope that you, too, will step out on faith to receive what God has in store for you.

I am blessed.

A Mother's Prayer

Heavenly Father, when I am in real distress I pray without reasoning. I just cry out to You, Lord, in my time of trouble and You save me from my distress.

Psalm 107:13 (personalized)

Father I come to You as a little child. I am asking for Your help. You said to ask and it shall be given, so now Lord I pray for each one of my children that You have given unto me.

I pray that they will have the will to love and follow You and You only. I pray for them to love others as their own selves. I pray for long life and good health so that they can do Your will and that they will prosper as their souls prosper.

I understand that I am just the vessel that brought them into the world. I know that they belong to You, Father, so when trouble comes concerning them and things get out of control, I can hand them over to You, Father. You and only You, Father, know them better than I do. You know the number of hairs that are on their heads--I don't.

Father, You said that You knew them before they were formed in my womb--Jeremiah 1:1 explains it all. Father, I pray that You will give me strength in their times of need and trouble because worrying brings on fear which makes room for the enemy to come in. I know that You did not give me a spirit of fear but of love, joy and a sound mind.

John 16:23 says "In that day you will ask nothing of me. Most assuredly, I say to you, whatever you ask the Father in my name, He will give it to you."

I stand on these words, Father--if I am saved then my whole household will be saved. So, thank you, Father, now and forever more. In Jesus Name, I pray. Amen.

My mother, Annie Marie Davis

October 26, 2009

Contents

Stage 1:

When I was a child:
I spoke like a child…

Chapter 1

Born to a child

On March 25, 1969, a year after Dr. Martin Luther King, Jr., was shot and killed, I was born at the Carolina Medical Center in Charlotte, North Carolina. My mother was 17 years old. It was not the best time to be the new kid on the block.

People were was still upset and angry, feelings were pent up. There was mass hysteria and people were very emotional during these years. At the time the only positive phenomenon was the Jackson 5:they were worldwide stars and they belonged to us.

My mother, Annie Marie Jackson, was a short lady, dark in skin tone, who had a striking resemblance to Diana Ross. She was the oldest of my grandmother's children and I'm the oldest grandchild in the hierarchy of the family.

Apparently, my grandmother was not at all pleased that her 16 year-old daughter was pregnant and not married. My grandmother had given birth to my Uncle Kenny just months before, and then, when I turned two years old, she would have my Uncle Tony You see, my grandmother was still in the process of having her own kids. Obviously upset over my grandmother's reaction, my mother went to live with my father's mother, Corrine Barnett. My father, Henry Martin Barnett, was short also, and worked at John Miller and Association, an office furniture delivery business on Hawthorne Lane.

He was a very short-tempered man who spent his days off talking on the CB radio--Grasshopper was his CB "handle"--or went fishing. Guess you can picture my untimely arrival to such young parents with no money and pretty much no plans for the future.

I was named Spencer Lee Jackson, (which changed to Spencer Lee Barnett at the age of six)---after my grandfather Charles Lee Jackson. He was a self employed tree man, that preached ownership. He believed that you should work hard for yourself, and build your own wealth, although he was not rich.

I was a big baby at nine pounds ten ounces--no hair and recurring eye problems. I was not pleased when my brother, Marvin Barnett was born, because I had all the toys to myself, and all the attention---but I was a lonely child. I used to talk to myself, and created pretend friends. But on the upside, I now had someone to play with, and could pass the blame on to---when things were broken. He was born two years after me. At that time, my parents moved us into a small two-bedroom apartment,

#3, on Siegle Avenue: the streets of North Charlotte would become familiar.

Guess my parents were doing OK because I recall being able to go to the Burger House on Fridays and getting that $1.00 every week as pocket money. Back then you could go to Josh's Store to buy a drink, a candy bar and bag full of the cookies--which they took out by hand--you could get two for a penny.

My Little sister, Shakeena G. Barnett, was born a few years after Marvin, I remember not being very happy about another kid coming along—another addition to the family. Plus, she was very light in color. I was thinking, "Who is this white baby?"

One day I was upstairs minding my own business, and this little baby started crying. I called out to my mom, who was downstairs playing cards—spades--with my Aunt Charlie or "Chicken." Don't ask.

My mother didn't reply, so I turned to this baby and said, "What are you looking at?" I decided I would pick her up for just a minute. I was holding her out at arm's length and gazed at her, then she started smiling at me.

At that point I thought, "This baby is not so bad," and decided I would now call her Keena--not Little Baby. After all, she was my sister.

I loved spending time with my brother Marvin and sister Keena. Because Keena was still a baby, she loved it when I make her laugh. I looked after her a lot, and she loves it when we played peek-a-boo! She would stay quiet when I cover my eyes with my hands--till I say peek-a-boo and uncovered my eyes. She would burst out with the sweet baby laugh each time. The other game she loves is when I tickle her all over.

"Where's Keena?" I would pretend to say, "Here comes the Tickle monster---and I'm going to tickle you all over!" She would laugh so much, when I tickle her feet, arms and belly, sometimes she ends up with the hiccups.

Whenever she laughed it fills the house with so much warmth and joy.

With my brother Marvin, who was a few years older than Keena---he looked up to me, and followed me everywhere I went.

We would play tips, you're in—chasing each other around till one is caught, then vice versa. Hide and go seek was another game we enjoyed. Both trying to outdo the other in finding the best hiding places.

We would be digging for bugs and insects in the back yard. Sometimes finding grasshoppers and keeping it in a jar, feeding it with blades of grass, and letting it go when we found something else to put in its place.

We unsuccessfully attempted to catch a colorful butterfly one time for Keena to look at. Our homemade net to catch the butterfly, kept getting caught in the tree branches each time we tried to swoop in on the butterfly.

We were able to catch lightning bugs in Jars and watched them light up under the covers while we were in the bed at night, until my mother would look in and see the covers lighting up, and would make us put them away.

When Marvin was a little older, he enjoyed playing with my friends and I, skate boarding, with our home made ramps in the parking lot. I had a yellow skate board made of fiber-glass.

I recall both Marvin and Keena showed a lot of respect for me as their older brother and someone they looked up to.

I love my brother and sister.

Chapter 2

800 pounds

Throughout my childhood I was very active, I loved playing marbles and trading them with my friends, trying to see who could collect the most.

I remember listening to Disco Duck, Planet Rock, and Kungfu Fighting around the clock--well until my dad's eight track player broke. Then he would listen to WGIV all day and night---no Television during this time.

The big wheel was the thing to have until they came out with the Green Machine—that was a bad ride. I never had one, but my cousin Charles did, and I stole it every chance I could. He'd be all over the place looking for it, and I would be all the way down at little Hornets Park pretending like it was mine in front of the kids there.

There were two brothers, Fred and Phil, who lived on the left end of the apartment building with their grandmother. We called her Nanny. My brother and I were good friends with them, but we still had our share of problems.

One particular day, one minute we were riding our bicycles, jumping homemade ramps, the next minute we were throwing punches. There were numerous pot holes in the parking lot, because the landlord was too cheap to fix anything—but, of course, he was always on time to collect your rent payment.

Anyway, the boys and I were jumping this ramp and the board came off. I went over and put it back,on the bricks that was holding it up. Fred then rode his bike up on the ramp. The board fell over and the ramp collapsed halfway through his jump. He flipped over the front of the bicycle, landing heavily on the ground and scraping his arms.

Marvin, Phil and I couldn't keep from laughing because, for sure, Fred would always laugh if we took a spill. He was livid and came in my direction.

"You were the one who fixed it," he said angrily. "Maybe you did it on purpose so I would get hurt."

He wanted to cause a fight, walking towards me with clenched fists. I began backing up.

"I didn't do anything," I said. "You just can't jump right."

He continued running towards me swinging his arms wildly.

"Stop," I warned him, but he had his mind made up.

He persisted in swinging madly at me, so I began to swing back at him, hitting him square in the nose. Blood gushed out of his nose. He was wiping it off with the back of his hand while he continued trying to fight me.

"You'd better stop," I said, "or I'm going to hit you again."

He finally realized that his nose was bleeding and could not carry on fighting.

"We will finish this fight one day soon," he said.

"I look forward to it," I said as we departed.

A few days later we were friends again, like nothing ever happened.

One day, soon after, we were outside cutting flips on an old mattress that someone had put on the curb for trash pick-up when we heard the loud sounds of fire trucks roaring down the road and heading to the top of the hill near Josh's Store.

We all looked at each other and began running up the hill past the other kids playing kick ball in the open field.

Once we got there, we all climbed on top of the red wall that stood in front of the house on the corner to get a better view of what all the commotion was about.

The fire trucks and police had stopped in front of Bo Bo's house. Bo Bo was an overweight guy that no one had seen in several years.

"Bo Bo died," we overheard someone say. "They can't move him out of the house because he's too big."

A few minutes later a huge crane on wheels came down the road, and the firemen took their axes and began pounding on the front walls of the house to knock it down and make it wider.

It seemed as they were going to take the entire front off of the house, knocking and pounding on it for close to twenty minutes—I ended up taken a seat on the grass because my legs begin to hurt. Phil had gone into Josh store and purchased some cookies and we were eating them.

We watched the crane lift Bo Bo out of the house and lay him onto the back of the rollback truck. Bo Bo's body was respectfully covered with sheets that they had taken from the house. No one really knew his actual weight, but it was rumored to be around eight hundred pounds.

I was always amazed at the phenomenal amount Bo Bo had eaten--to the point he could no long come out the house or even walk at all.

For some time after this, I wouldn't finish my food. I was thinking that maybe I would get big like that.

"Bo Bo had an eating disorder and health problems," my mother said one day. "You have no worries, Spencer, you can eat like a normal person."

I didn't know what that meant back then, but she said I would be OK, and I believed her.

Chapter 3

Going out for cigarettes

My life on Siegle Avenue was a time when things were just simple. My parents were together; we had a car and a phone--which was rare--and I had no idea we were poor.

One day I walked up the street to the church on the corner, hanging a left down 20th Street where my grandmother lived. My aunt Linda was gathering all of the kids together to take us to the Cordelia Swimming pool on Davidson Street.

We were to go swimming and then wait anxiously for the "free lunch" trucks to come--these were trucks offering free lunches to kids in the summertime. I remember some kid kept telling me that he knew my daddy. I did not think much about it; I was too busy trying to keep my place in line.

A few days passed by and my dad took us to Bill's Barber Shop on Davidson Street to get the same hair cut we had received for years--dark temper with a part. As soon as we were done having our hair cut, while watching Bill eat those sunflower seeds that he always seemed to spit on the floor. He would miss the trash can, but offer me a job to come after hours and sweep it all up. No thanks!

On the way home we detoured down Allen Street and came to a stop in front of a house. My dad blew the horn and some skinny lady that I had noticed around the neighborhood came to the door.

They talked for a few minutes. Then, the same little boy that, just days before, had made it his point to let me know he knew my dad, came out from behind the lady. He walked outside, looked at me and began to play with a yellow tanker truck laying in the front yard. I heard my dad tell the lady he would be back and we went home.

Inside the house, my mom was changing my little sister's smelly butt. Holding my nose, I took a seat on the old brown chair that had been in the house all my life and started watching Rin Tin Tin.

"I have to run back out and get some cigarettes," my dad told my mom.

I was very puzzled as to why he told my mom he was going out for cigarettes when he had clearly told the skinny lady he was coming back.

He went out and was gone for some time. My mom began to wonder why he was gone so long.

“Where is he?” she said to no one in particular.

I was still watching TV—now it was The Lone Ranger—and looked up.

“Well,” I said, “maybe you should ring the skinny lady’s house.”

My mom looked surprised and puzzled at same time asked,

“What skinny lady?” she said.

“You know…the one that lives on Allen Street,” I said.

“No,” she said sharply and seriously. She went across the parking lot to Apartment #5, my Aunt Chicken’s. They came back looking very solemn about what it was they were going to do next.

Being a kid I didn’t think much about it at the time, but I had just betrayed my dad and dobbed him in.

My mother asked me to show them where the house was located. We started out, up the road to Allen Street, and arrived at the house.

I pointed to the door the skinny lady had come out of. My Aunt started knocking on door. The same little boy--who I had seen enough of for one week--opened the door.

I heard my mother ask if my father was there, knowing very well he was because his red Pontiac LeMans—with the rusty top—was parked in front.

I had just seen my mother walk over and touch its hood, check to see if it was still warm.

"Yes," the little boy said and opened the screen door--which had no screen in it-- and we went inside.

No one was visible, so we continued our way to the back rooms. I wandered into a little room on the left my mother had passed by. What I saw next tainted me for a lot of my childhood years.

My dad was shamelessly lying naked in the bed, with the skinny lady. Before I could turn and exit, my mother was there standing behind me.

My mother took a deep breath.

"Go outside," she told me.

As I left the room, I looked back at my father who had gotten up by this point and was trying to retrieve his clothes. He gave me this cold stare and I turned away.

I heard a lot of yelling and screaming as I made my way outside. When I reached the front yard, I saw the little boy with his yellow truck.

"Would you like to play?" the little boy asked.

"Fine," I said.

Being kids, we didn't think much about what was going on inside. A few minutes later my mother and aunt stormed back outside. My mother was clearly upset and pulled out a Newport cigarette with trembling hands. Tears streaked her face. My aunt was doing her best, trying to calm her down.

My mother all of a sudden looked at me and the boy playing. We were friends now

"Get away from him," she yelled. "Let's go.

On our slow journey back home, I became even more confused.

"I don't want you to ever playing with him again," she said as we walked. I couldn't understand why I was not allowed to be his friend.

It seemed as if the walk home lasted forever. My mom cried like I had never seen before. I watched helplessly as my Aunt put a comforting arm around my mother's shoulders. I knew at that moment, things will never be the same again for us.

She made my dad move out the next day. For the next 7 years I blamed myself for telling--even if I didn't realize at the time I was telling.

I hated my father for breaking up the family and making my mother cry. For the rest of my childhood, we would go to my father's place on the weekends, at different locations because he moved around a lot.

I hated it.

When I turned 15, I had a choice to go or not. I always chose not to go.

My relationship with my father would never be the same

I barely spoke to him for the next 21 years.

Chapter 4

So many pennies

After my father was banned from my mother's life, money got tough. We didn't get that Washington $1.00 every week anymore. My mother was on her own, and though my father was sending $100 a month, with three kids, it was not much. My brother and I could go through that amount in food alone. On top of that were clothes for us and diapers for my little sister--but most of all, what money there was did not cover paying the bills.

One day, on the bus going home from school, a friend who lived on the corner of Siegle Avenue and 20th Street, in front of the church, invited me over to his house to play on Saturday.

"I'll have to ask my mother when I get home," I said.

"OK," he said, "just come over, if you can, around noon."

When we arrived at my bus stop, I got off and walked down the hill to my parking lot, kicking rocks. I heard a loud noise coming over the hill top, so I turned and looked back up the road.

A gold Chevy SS belonging to my neighbor came speeding over the hilltop, making a hard left turn into the parking lot. I had to run to avoid being hit by this crazy driver.

Now it had always being rumored that this neighbor was a bank robber. I didn't know if it was true, but one night when I was at the top of my stairs I heard my parents and their friends talking about him as they played cards. They were going on about him always having money, never working, and looking like someone in the wanted posters they had seen on the news. But no one was ever really sure if it was him or not.

Anyway, I looked back at him quickly and turned away because I wasn't going to look or even dare to stare him down. I had been told by the other kids this man hated people staring at him.

I went inside my apartment, breathing a little heavy, almost breathless from my brush with death.

My mother was sitting at the kitchen table looking at the huge, never-ending stack of bills. She turned to me.

"That fool driving fast again?" she said.

“Yes,” I said.

“You OK?”

“Yes,” I said. ”What are you doing?”

“Paying bills,” she said.

“I can try to cut grass to get some money to help you pay the bills,” I said.

“Son,” she said, smiling, “you’re 7 years old. You’ll have plenty of time to pay bills later. But, thank you for asking.”

“By the way,” I said, “can I go over to Tony’s house tomorrow and play?

“After all your chores are done tomorrow, you may be excused to go,” she said.

The next morning I was up bright and early, eagerly working on my chores trying to get them done so that I would have more time to play over at Tony’s house.

I finished my list and approached my mother, who was outside, hanging clothes on the clothes line at the back of the house.

She was having problems hanging the white sheets, so I grabbed an end of the sheet and held it until she could put her end over the string that ran from pole to pole. Then she pinned the sheet, fixing it tight with these little wooden clothespins.

Once she got the first end up she came and grabbed my side of the sheet because I was too short to hang it myself.

"All of my chores are done." I said, "Can I go over to Tony's house now?

"Go have a bowl of Sugar Smacks and then you can go," she said. "But be careful crossing the road and be back in two hours."

I hurried back inside and poured a very small amount of cereal in a bowl, added milk and started eating it. I literally stuffed the cereal down my throat and rushed out the door. I stopped at the edge of the road looked up and down the street. When it was clear of cars, I ran across and up the hill to Tony's house.

I excitedly approached his doorsteps and knocked. An older girl answered the door in her night gown. I wasn't sure who she was, but I didn't think it was Tony's mother because she didn't look old enough to be a mother.

"It's pretty early to be paying a visit, don't you think?" she said.

I didn't say anything, but I was thinking, "It's 11:45AM and seems like an OK time to me."

She pushed open the screen door and waved me in, scratching on her rear end as she turned her back to me, closing and latching the screen door.

I went into the little room on the left where I saw Tony standing with a Stretch Armstrong man in his hands.

Tony had so many toys in that room and we played with everything. I was constantly thinking, "How does he have so many toys?"

"Do you want to go down to the basement and play with my other toys?" he asked.

I looked at him in disbelief.

"You have more toys?" I said.

"Yes," he said. "Follow me." Which I did--of course!

I followed Tony down a little stairway to this dark and old-smelling room with broken window panes. There were toys everywhere. I couldn't believe it. My eyes opened wide in amazement. I was thinking, "This kid must be as rich as Ritchie Rich from television."

There were pennies in these big clear glass jars everywhere and what appeared to be thousands more scattered all over the basement floor.

"Why you have so much money down here?" I said.

""I don't know," he said, "but you can have some."

"'I looked at him, even more surprised, and tried to digest what he said.

"Really…?" I said.

"Yes," he said.

I was thinking, "Maybe I can help my mother pay the bills with some of these pennies."

I began to pick the pennies up, putting them in my pocket, totally forgetting to play. I eagerly picked up the pennies from the floor and put them into my pockets, totally oblivious to Tony who wanted to continue playing. He was wrestling me, but I continued to pick up the pennies, even while he was on my back.

The lady came to the top of the stairs.

"Someone is at the door for you," she called down to me.

I went upstairs to see who it was. It was my Aunt Peaches who was on her way to my grandmother's. My mother had asked her sister to stop by Tony's and tell me to come home.

I said goodbye to Tony, hugged my Auntie and ran home. I arrived with my pockets heavily loaded down with pennies, both the front ones and a small amount in my left back pocket.

My mother stared at me.

"What's in your pockets?" she said.

“Pennies,” I said.

“Where did you get them from?” she said.

“From Tony’s house,” I said. “They were all over the floor and he said I could have some. I was thinking you can use them for the bills.”

She was very upset and visibly disappointed in me.

“That is stealing,” she said, “and you don’t steal from people.”

After my punishment, a very,very long and painful spanking, she marched me back to Tony’s house with the pennies in a brown paper bag. She knocked on the door and the same lady answered the door, this time she had rollers in her hair, but was still in her nightgown---eating a honey bun.

“Can I help you?” the lady asked.

“My son, Spencer, has something he wants to say to you,” she told the lady and turned to me.

I looked up unwillingly, and ashamed about what I had done.

“I took something that doesn’t belong to me and I’m very sorry,” I said. Awkwardly, I held out my hands with the bag of pennies in them.

The lady seized the bag from my hands, opened it, and looked inside.

"Your son told him it was OK to take them," my mother said, "but I know it was not."

"He's not my son," the lady said. "He's my little brother."

"OK," my mother said to the lady in the night gown, "tell your mother that I am very sorry and my son won't ever do it again."

We turned away and headed back home. While we walked, my mother began educating me about stealing.

"I know what your intentions were," my mother said as we neared home, "but I don't want you to ever steal to help someone, because as you help one, you also hurt another."

"OK," I said, feeling disgraced. "I am very sorry."

Chapter 5

The big black frying pan

One sunny day as I was enjoying myself riding my bicycle in the parking lot on Siegle Avenue, I heard my mother call from within our apartment. I got off the bicycle and raced inside.

"Did you call me?" I said.

"Yes," she said. "Change the television."

I just stood looking at her.

I thought "Is she serious?" She was lying on the old brown chair and the TV was less than 3 feet away.

"Ride your bicycle up to your grandmother's and ask her if I can use her big black frying pan," she said. A big black pan was the Cadillac of frying pans. I was a little confused.

"But we have many pans here," I said.

"I need that one to make your favorite," she said, smiling.

Within two seconds, I raced out the door and grabbed my bicycle.

I could hear my mom's crisp laughter from inside the house at the way I reacted to her words. My stomach rumbled with hunger at the thought of her making my most favorite food. I knew she was going to make my birthmark-food:cornbread. I could eat it all day, plain or accompanied with other food--but it was the ultimate when eaten with chili beans.

My stomach gurgled again and again with sheer delight. I dashed up the road to my grandmother's house. Still breathing heavily from my vigorous peddling up the hill and then down 20th Street, I must have made it there in less than five minutes.

Catching my breath, I walked up on the porch where my grandmother's lazy brother John Dee sat with his drinking buddy, Pye June.

Both were drenched in their own sweat from sitting in the sun, so drunk that they were immobilized on the spot. Neither of them cared or was able to shift out of the sweltering heat.

"Give me a dollar, boy!" they drunkenly yelled as I passed by.

Since I was just a kid and did not have any money to give them to support their daily habit of drinking and being intoxicated before noon, I kept walking.

I spotted my Grandmother crouching in her hiding place. Whenever she felt a storm was coming, she got in a small closet in the hallway and left the door slightly opened. You see, she was afraid of thunder and lightning. Visualize in your mind a grandmother huddled up, terrified in a tiny closet, waiting for the thunder and lightning to stop.

I walked to the door.

"Mama," I whispered.

"Yes," she said.

"My mommy told me to come and ask you if she can use your big black frying pan," I said.

"Run along to the kitchen," she said. "Look under the cabinets and get the pan."

I went into the kitchen to retrieve the pan and returned to the closet door to show her that I had indeed found it.

"I guess your mom is going to make you some cornbread," she said.

"Yes, Ma," I said and gave her an ecstatic smile.

"Fetch me my pocketbook on the bed," she said.

I picked it up and handed it to her, sliding it through the slit in the closet door. She rummaged around in the pocketbook among the many papers and things inside and gave me a dollar.

"Take this dollar and buy yourself something after you have eaten your dinner. Now hurry home and look out for cars. I sense a storm coming," she said.

I could tell she was worried.

"Thank you, Mama," I said.

I went back outside into the blistering heat, once again confronted by the two drunks who asked me for a dollar. I took the dollar—just given to me by my grandmother seconds before-- out of my pocket. I handed it to Uncle John Dee.

He snatched it out of my hand and attempted to get up. He plummeted back down on the chair and looked up at me.

"You keep it," he said, his drunken speech was slurred. "I've had enough to drink for one day."

Without hesitation, I grabbed the dollar, got on my bicycle and peddled back home—all the time gripping the big black frying pan.

I arrived home, handed the frying pan to my mother, and patiently watched her make the cornbread.

"Fetch me two eggs from the fridge please." She said while whisking the batter manually.

“Why aren’t you using the electric mixer?” I asked.

“You don’t mix cornbread with an electric mixer” My mother replied, “You don’t want the batter too thin, you just need to get the lumps out.”

Once she finished whisking, and after I greased the pan with a stick of butter---she poured the batter in, and placed it in the oven.

I never understood the purpose of needing a big black frying pan, but, in the end, every batch of cornbread made from that big black frying pan--without a doubt--produced the perfect delicious cornbread.

Chapter 6

Innocence lost

While teaching art at Villa Heights Elementary on Pinckney Avenue during the day, my mother was a manager at Woolworth's Department Store in the evenings.

My mother was burdened with a lot after separating from my dad, but she refused to go back to him. As a result, we spent a lot of time with a cousin who I will call Feet--she had very big feet for a girl.

I remember clearly one particular night when Feet--then a 16 year-old girl—was babysitting us. It was a pretty normal night like it had always been before: we watched TV, had a few cookies for a snack and a glass of red Kool-Aid, before going off to bed.

I woke up suddenly, from a deep sleep, feeling movement on the bed. Eyes half-opened, I noticed

Feet shifting my brother to the other bed in the room which was occupied by my little sister.

Feet returned to sit beside me.

"Are you a big boy?" she asked, rubbing my leg.

"Yes, I'm a big boy," I said, still half asleep.

"I believe you," she said, "because you have a big wiener."

I lay there, lost in confusion, as Feet played with my body. I felt strangely uncomfortable. I wasn't sure what Feet got out of doing this, but her performance was repeated, frequently after that night, always ending with her telling me not to tell anyone about her special little treat for me.

Because my mother had to work on some Saturdays, there were times when Feet looked after us during the day.

"Go and play with your little sister downstairs," she told my little brother one Saturday. She tempted them with snacks when it was clearly not snack time.

Alone with me, she began performing her strange acts as she had always done, but this time she went further, removing all of her clothes and mine as well.

She lay on her back and demanded I get on top of her. I obeyed.

I remember being mortified by the stench of her breath, tasting and smelling like tobacco.

I hated it. I was eight years old.

These indecent episodes continued, occurring frequently, but I never told anyone. I didn't know if I was scared or if I liked it. I definitely did not understand it.

I didn't know if telling would matter, or if anyone would believe me. After I became a teenager, I would see her from time to time. She would forever give me a sinister look, as if she still wanted me.

This same kind of incident happened to me again with a family friend who was looking after us. She went by the name of Cookie. It must have been about six months after a last encounter with Feet.

Cookie was babysitting us one night and she told me to go upstairs to get a diaper for Shakeena, my little sister.

I couldn't find one, so she came upstairs and appeared to be looking around for it.

I had my back turned to her when she surprised me by wrapping her arms around me.

"Are you my boyfriend?" she asked.

I was totally puzzled.

"I guess so," I said.

Then she turned me around, began kissing me and touching me. I remember her breathing heavily and removing my clothes.

"Here we go again," I was thinking.

She pushed me back on my mother's bed and made me touch her in an improper manner. I was scared she will get upset with me, if I didn't obey her.

I felt discomfort, and was distressed at the thought of it happening again.

Then my little sister started crying.

Cookie hastily got dressed, and ordered me to get dressed too.

"It's a secret," she said before leaving to attend to my sister. "You better not tell anyone or you will be in big trouble."

After she left, I went to the bathroom and washed my hands.

I kept quiet.

People may think lewd and indecent acts of sexual abuse to young and innocent boys are rare, but it happens often. It is rare to hear about—because of the threats to silence the victims at the time of the abuse.

I was only eight years old. I didn't understand what these incidents would do to my life.

I didn't understand that later on, in my early adult years, I would develop a negative attitude towards women.

I never told anyone about this part of my life until I was 39 years old.

Chapter 7

January 1979

Being nine years old was a great time in my life--what I had experienced before was more than enough for a life time. I just wanted to be a normal kid for now: no cheating dad, fights or sex as a kid.

For the time being everything was back to normal—well as best it could get. I put the things that happen in the back of my head for now and tried to pretend they didn't happen—and for awhile I did forget.

I loved life, hanging out with my cousin, Charles Jackson, my uncles Kenny and Tony, and my brother Marvin. We would be up to mischief as any normal kids would. We did things kids did in the early 80's---fixing our bikes, building club houses and hating girls.

We went to the Dilworth Movie Theater one Saturday to watch Bruce Lee---$1.00. After being mesmerized by two Bruce Lee movies in a row, we came out all jacked up thinking we knew karate.

We were full of energy, kicking, jumping, and making the hitting sounds. I was wondering about the next day, what I was going to do, having spent all the money we had earned that day cutting grass.

We made it back to my grandmother's house and my uncle, Oscar Agurs, was there. He looked sharp with his army suit on. My Uncle Oscar became part of the family when he married my Aunt Patricia. I idolized him during my childhood years: he was a smart and organized man. I wanted to grow up and achieve my dreams, be smart and organized just like him.

I heard Uncle Oscar saying that he would be home for the weekend and was going to watch football the next day. I didn't know much about football then, but I knew if he liked it, well, it must be cool.

So the next day, I waited impatiently to see what the big deal was about---this football thing. The men in family were gathered around the Television eating and having a good laugh. My grandmother cooked fried chicken, cabbage, cornbread and sweet tea. I could smell the aroma of the food which lingered around the house. To me she was the best cook in the world. My Uncles were engaged in a friendly tease about each other's teams, while waiting for the game to start.

All of the kids were heading outside to play. Some of the girls were playing hop scotch while others were engaged in skipping rope.

The boys were building a tree house, which did not appear sturdy or safe. After hearing the kids laughing joyfully outside, I peeped out the window. I wanted to join the boys and build the tree house, but I was also curious about this football game—so I stayed.

Finally this game comes on and there were two teams playing--the Dallas Cowboys and the Pittsburgh Steelers.

"Which team do you like best?" I asked my uncles.

All of a sudden the room erupted with everyone talking at once, debating which team was better. They were all fond of their own teams and proud to defend them to the end. I noticed a few of them, slapping each other on the back, for defending their team—or giving each other hi-fives.

The room was split evenly. No one was letting the other out-talk another about which team was best. My inquisitive mind was thinking…and thinking.

I knew that Dallas colors were cool, but the Steelers were tough. I liked the Dallas Star on the helmet, but Steelers had Franco Harris. Dallas had the prettiest cheerleaders I had ever seen, but the Steelers won the game. Very interesting.

"What team should I like?" I asked my Uncle Oscar. I thought because he was a Cowboys fan, he would want me to be like him, and like Cowboys too.

"Whichever team you pick," he said, "you have to really like them, support them and be proud of them throughout the good and bad times. But, most of all, you have to defend them till the end."

Right then, I knew it had to be Dallas because I loved everything about them. After all, they were America's Team.

Go Dallas!

Chapter 8

Who will protect my son?

Sometimes life deals you situations that are out of your control---or you're just too young to understand what's going on.

I remember one Saturday night at the end of March. I knew it was March because I had just turned nine years old on 25th of that month. My mother was down at the Blue Mist Lounge with my cousin, Joanne, and her boyfriend, Willie-Mo.

Aunt Carolyn was babysitting me and my siblings---I don't know why because she was just three years older than me.

Aunt Carolyn had fallen asleep early saying she was tired from dancing at the disco at Belmont Center earlier that evening. Plus, she said, she didn't want to go home and face the wrath of my grandmother who hadn't given her permission to attend the disco.

I couldn't sleep. I went downstairs and started eating on some Boston Baked Beans and a Jack's "Rocky n' Roll" cookie with the white icing on top. I was watching The Twilight Zone.

I heard a noise outside so I got up to look. I dropped the box of Boston Baked Beans on the floor. They rolled all over and under the old brown chair.

Moving the curtain back from the front door window, I peered outside and noticed Lenny walking across the parking lot. I assumed he was cutting through the alleyway between the apartment buildings to get to his house quicker, which was across the street from my apartment.

I knew it was Lenny because he had dated my Auntie Linda before, and I knew the way he walked. He was a very cool guy with wavy hair and he always had a story to tell.

Then---out of nowhere---two other guys ran up behind him and start hitting him and trying to drag him to the ground. But Lenny was very strong and could fight well for his size. Although, he must have been only about 120 pounds then, he was actually winning the fight against the two guys.

I pushed the curtain closed and just peeped out because I didn't want them to see me looking. I was only nine and these guys looked like they could have been 18 to 20. They seemed very scary to me.

I knew one of the other guys who was fighting with Lenny because I used to see him sitting on a porch on Pegram Street. I never knew his name, but I would hear people call him Doughboy.

After Lenny seemed to have gotten them to the point of not wanting to fight him anymore, he turned to walk across the street to his house. Doughboy got up off the ground and pulled something shiny out of his back left pocket. He pointed the object towards Lenny's back and I saw a cloud of smoke come from it.

Shocked, I fell backwards into the living room, hitting my head on the corner of the wall that led upstairs. I jumped back up wanting to see what happened to Lenny. I saw him lying in the middle of the street and I saw Doughboy walking closer to him, pointing the shiny thing—which, by now, I knew was a gun.

He put the gun at Lenny's back, about to shoot him again, but then a car came over the hill, startling Doughboy. He turned and ran between the apartments. The car stopped just inches from where Lenny lay, but they didn't get out and help him. They simply pulled around and continued down the road.

I turned and ran upstairs, my heart pounding a hundred miles an hour, to wake my Aunt Carolyn.

"Wake up, wake up, Auntie Carolyn," I cried, yelling and pulling on her. "Lenny's hurt and he needs help." Breathlessly barely getting my words out.

She jumped up started down the stairs, me right on her heels, her hair rollers falling out as we reached the bottom steps. She pulled the door open, but by this time Lenny was not in sight.

Aunt Carolyn ran across the parking lot to use my Aunt Chicken's phone because our phone had been disconnected due to non-payment.

A little while later the police arrived. By then, most of the neighbors were awakened by the gunshot, and were outside gossiping about what might have happened---but they were all wrong.

I stood quietly as the police entered Lenny's house. A few minutes later they surfaced and I heard one officer tell the other to radio in for a homicide detective. I knew from watching Perry Mason that "homicide" is who they call when someone is dead.

Sure enough, Lenny was dead. I heard it announced by the officer who was asking if anyone had seen what happened.

I stood quietly as my mother--who had arrived home after hearing people in the lounge, saying someone was killed on Siegle Avenue—was talking with my Aunt Carolyn. My Aunt gave her the details I had previously shared with her.

My Aunt Linda was there now, having heard the news from Cookie who was her best friend. I knew she was sad because she still cared for Lenny dearly. I could see the hurt on her face.

My mother pulled me to the side, soothing my back with the gentle caress of her hand and asked me if I was ok.

"Yes" I said.

"Would you be OK telling the policeman what your saw?" she asked me. "No kid should see so much, but you need to tell the police who did this. No one deserves to die like Lenny died. I love you and I am sorry I wasn't home with you tonight."

"Lenny was always nice to me," I said. I was sad he had to die. "I want them to go to jail."

My mother walked over to the officers and let them know I had valuable information that would help them catch Lenny's killer.

"I don't want anyone to know of this for the protection of my child and my other kids," she told them.

The officer agreed to meet my mother and me later at The Dairy Cream Ice Cream Shop on Central Avenue.

We arrived at the shop---long closed because by now it was 3:20AM. I was allowed to sit in the front seat of the police car. I was amazed at all of the gadgets inside.

I was thinking, "Maybe I could be a police officer when I grow up."

While my mother stood next to my side of the car door, I told what I had witnessed. An officer stood beside my mother taking my statement. The officer said I might have to testify in court and point out the shooter.

"No way," my mother, a very protective soul, said. "You guys will not be around every day to protect my son. He is here to give you a statement because I want him to know Lenny didn't deserve to die this way."

"But," my mother continued, "I am not about to let my son be put through a trial and risk his life as well. Are we done now? Can we leave now?"

I got out of the officer's car and back into the car of a neighbor who had driven us up to meet the officers.

I didn't understand what the court stuff was then, but my mother told me that I had done the right thing.

"But, but that was as far as we will go," she said. "I will not risk your life for anyone.

I just looked at her.

"OK," I said.

Then I turned to look at the billboard announcing the up-coming wresting match at the Grady Cole Center between Rick Flair and Andre The Giant.

Lenny's killer was never arrested because the officers didn't really care to pursue the case. But we heard a few months later, Doughboy was gunned down at Little Hornet's Store over a dice game.

Karma caught up with him.

Chapter 9

Why Would They Care?

I remember attending a little white church down off Belmont Avenue on 15th street: Good Shepherd Baptist Church. It was an old building that always seemed to require some kind of repairs and the roof would leak often. I remember sometimes when it rained we would move to another seat, to keep dry--listening to the Preacher as the drip, drip of the rain came down hitting the edge of the pews and rolling onto the carpet. I always wondered what they did with the church building fund.

Still we attended regularly, not caring what needed to be renovated, just as long as we went.

It was an all black church except for the preacher, Mr. Crocker and his wife. Most of the people in the church were related to me in some kind of way—a cousin, an aunt or uncle.

I was puzzled as to why these white people would come to the black neighborhood to teach us about the Bible. I mean, why would they even care? Didn't they have a Church in their own neighborhood to teach about the bible? Nevertheless, they came for years and actually appeared genuine about being there. They never gave up on the people. They were dedicated to the people in our community. Never once did I see a glimpse of hopelessness in their eyes. Always smiling and guiding us, teaching us, to look for God in times of need.

I learned not to judge a book by its cover. I also knew that people really cared for one another back then and would help others out in a time of need. There were time when my mother would feed the neighbors kids because they didn't have any money one week, or borrowing sugar or bread from each other.

The church would teach me a lot about sharing and reaching out to others. And I learn of how it all began and how Jesus was born.

I learned that Jesus was born in Bethlehem in a barn and placed in a manger, due to shortage of accommodation. I was mesmerized by Jesus informing his disciples he would suffer, and die before being resurrected within three day's time. I learned he sacrificed himself in order for me to live. Jesus had surrendered his life when he had no faults, or ill will against anyone—even to those that had betrayed him. I was taught that He is always with me and will never leave me. I was extremely into the Bible, eager and willing to learn all I could. I was very fascinated with the stories of the Bible, always yearning to learn every element of it.

I wanted to pray all my grief away, but many times I got irritated with God for not providing me everything I asked for---not realizing, I received what I needed. I am blessed to have a roof over my head, food on the table, and clothes on my back. I learned that you have to step out on faith and give all things to God: Hurry up and Wait. Be ready. Be prepared. Wait on God to give you the map.

Many times in life my faith would being challenged, but I never believed that God would leave me. I would use Jesus's crucifixion as my inspiration to continue on. Today, I know that if my mother hadn't kept persisting and making me attend church from an early age, I wouldn't have had any kind of guidance to live by.

Even then, I appreciated this strict nurturing that would keep me level-headed in times of trouble. There wasn't anything in life that could outshine my good feeling. The Spirit of God touched me deep down in my soul; it lifted my feet off the ground and gave me such joy. I loved the Lord.

I recall one Sunday we were having service and the preacher was teaching us about being obedient to God and to our parents. I never liked that part because I was still upset with my dad and did not respect him enough to listen to the preacher, because I had become more distant and unapproachable, isolating myself from the father who had tainted my mind with hate.

I never believed that I would bond with my father ever again, and I found it hard to forgive him. This hatred for my father would span over many years of my life.

It would cost me dearly.

Chapter 10

The candy girl

After living on Siegle for 11 years, we moved to Tryon Terrace Apartments off North Tryon Street, in Apt. #3--something about the #3!

It was a three bedroom, so I was very happy to get my own room. I put up poster's that I ripped out of Right On and Jet magazines, I was very organized and didn't want my sister and brother to mess up my room—putting homemade DO NOT ENTER signs on the door with duck tape and thumb tacks.

We lived in a unit with four apartments on the row and were backed up to some woods that had a pathway leading to some recycling companies—that would buy aluminum cans by the weight. It would take weeks at a time just to save one bag and then you had to smash them flat, in order for them to take them, and then maybe you would get three dollars if you're lucky.

In the apartment to our right was a family of five: the parents, two girls and one little brother. On the other side was a single mother, two sons and one little daughter. (the McLaughlin's) We all got along very well. Most of the time, we all looked out for each other. But, then there was the rest of the neighborhood which was OK and to our liking.

Most of our days were filled with football, kickball, and fighting--lots of fighting, much more fighting than the average kids. I spent a lot of my free time hanging out in my room listening to my Prince and Spinner's records, singing into a homemade microphone---I couldn't sing--and imagining what I was going to buy with all the money that I would make when I became famous.

What really made me want to sing was seeing Elvis Presley on television---seeing how people seemed to love and adore him and stayed dedicated to his music throughout their lives. I always wondered what that would feel like--not to mention the leagues of screaming girls all wanting a piece of Elvis.

I also remember on weekends there would always be these block parties down behind the store. I remember this one band that played there all the time called The Dice Band---to me these guys were rock stars.

Across the parking lot from us was a big family of kids that lived with their grandmother---must have been at least 8 of them. There was this girl that lived there who caught my attention---we'll call her Tammy.

Well, Tammy was the prettiest girl I had ever seen up until that point in my life. She was very tall for a girl, light skin, and beautiful long hair. But, she always made me nervous and I was never able to talk when I would see her. I was too captivated by her beauty, to utter a word. I didn't want to spoil her prettiness. I was a wounded, lovesick young lad.

And to add salt to the open wound, she was dating this guy who pretty much was the football star of the neighborhood. I played sports, too, but I was nowhere near as good as this guy—and, to top it off, he was a very handsome boy.

I never really thought highly of myself, or as good looking. At the time I was also a shy boy. I used to hang around Tammy's brothers just to be able to catch a glimpse of her loveliness. I noticed she would always be eating a candy called Now & Later's. Interesting!

I got this bright idea that maybe I could buy her some candy and then maybe she would like me--the mind of a 11 year-old. Every time my mom would send me to the store to get bread, drink, or other groceries, I---being only 11 and with no job---would buy a pack of Now & Later's for 10 cents, hoping my mom didn't really count the change.

I would stop by Tammy's house and give them to whoever came to the door.

"These are for Tammy," I would say.

Sure enough it worked—or so I thought. She started being very nice to me, writing me notes and even holding my hand once---I know. Right.

I was on "cloud nine" at this point and you couldn't tell me anything: I was in love.

But the love was short lived. Things began to unravel in a terrible way. Not only was Tammy still someone else's girlfriend, she got braces and I got into a fight with her cousin one weekend.

Add all that up, plus the fact she was the bus monitor. She decided that since I fought her cousin on the weekend, she would write me up for talking on the bus, which was not true. The next day I had to go to detention after she reported me, I didn't even try to explain to the principal the truth.

Right then, I hated girls!

I began forming my own opinions about girls. I was starting to get very bad thoughts about them: Are they all like that? Will they all use me? Should I just use girls before they use me?

I was very hurt by this experience and didn't have the answers to my questions. Regardless of my lack of knowledge or understanding about girls, my mind was beginning to determine that they only used me.

Girls only wanted to take advantage of me. It was evident from the experiences with Feet, Cookie and now---the candy girl.

My 11 year-old heart was shattered.

Stage 2:

When I was a child:
I thought like a child,
I reasoned like a child…

Chapter 11

The house burned down

My mother began dating this guy named Larry Davis. He was 21 years old and she was 28 at the time. Now mind you, I was 12, so you can guess the weirdness in that at the time.

He was light skinned, handsome, and very mature for a 21 year-old. He had a job working for a parts supply company, called Sulliar, off of Clinton Road. He would always be talking about sports, making money--plus he was a heavy cigarette smoker.

I didn't think much of him. I had made my mind up about guys coming around and trying to play dad. Like any typical young protective teenager, I kept a close eye on him. After a while, my hatred for this guy subsided, and I observed that he seemed to be a very nice guy. He was always around to help my mother out with things my dad was never around to do. He minimized her heavy burdens, and, therefore, reduced her stress level.

I could see she loved his company; she seemed to be enjoying his help around the house, and she did appear a lot happier. I had to admit that someone who could make my mom smile again must be OK.

During this time, I was going to school at J.T. Williams Elementary and then on to Albemarle Road Middle School. One day, something out of the ordinary happened to me while I was at school.

I was walking the hallway in between classes, minding my own business, and this girl, who I always saw around the school, walked up to me and handed me a note. Then she walked away.

I watched her walk away, puzzled and anxious to see what was in the note. I excitedly opened the note and started reading. As I walked and read, I bumped into people and forgot the minimal amount of time we had in-between classes.

The note read:

My name is Kim. I think you are cute and handsome. Do you have a girlfriend? Would you like to go out with me? Yes__or__No Check one.

Try to remember, at this point, I was done with girls because I was devastated by one not too long before.

But, this was different: she liked me. There was no need to supply candy or compete with the jock.

I checked Yes and returned it to her before boarding the school bus at the end of the school day. I was on top of the world and was forming a new opinion about girls as I sat and daydreamed about her on the bus.

But, this happiness was very short-lived because when the bus stopped in front of my parking lot, I noticed fire trucks and police cars everywhere.

Dark clouds of smoke lingered in the air. You could smell and taste it in your mouth. As I got closer, I noticed it was my building that the smoke was coming from and, in fact, it was my apartment.

I saw my mother standing with my Aunt Patricia Agurs. I walked up to them.

"What happened?" I asked.

I was guided by my aunt back into the remains of the burnt down apartment to retrieve anything that wasn't burned.

As we made our way inside she told me that Larry had worked the night before and was home resting in bed. He fell asleep with a cigarette in his hand. The bed caught on fire and he had to jump from the 2nd floor out of the window.

I got to my room and there was nothing to retrieve--nothing. Everything special I owned was gone: my Chuck Taylor shoes, my glitter Michael Jackson glove---that I worked so hard on---and the Red Ryder BB gun.

All I could do was cry. Right then, I had an attitude with God about this. I felt he owed me.

I was thinking, “Why does God always make things happen to me? What have I done that’s so bad?” My Aunt Patricia noticed me crying and told me to pray to God for strength. I looked at her.

“I’m never praying again,” I said.

She grabbed me by my arm.

“Don’t you ever say that again,” she said. “God didn’t do this--the Devil did. Never let anything in life get you to the point where you want to abandon God because He will never leave you or forsake you.” She took my hand and we knelt down and prayed together.

We moved to Earle Village and lived with my grandmother in what we called the “brown apartments” on Caldwell Street---in front of First Ward School.

My mother and Larry moved in with his father behind West Charlotte High School.

I never saw Kim again.

Chapter 12

Mrs. Jackson in Earle Village

My grandmother, Maybelle Jackson, had lived in the brown apartments since I was about 10 years old. She had moved there from North Charlotte off 20th Street after she left my grandfather for having an affair. They never divorced.

I already knew most of the people living there and in the neighborhood. There were a lot of families and we had differences with them, but we would always make up just hours later.

Like any neighborhood you had the kids that never came outside until their mothers went to work, the church lady that everyone hated to see coming---funny because her son was the neighborhood drunk---and the lonely guy who pushed the buggy around full of his possessions that looked like junk, but meant the world to him.

My grandmother was a very friendly lady, a Christian, but didn't attend church much---she said her church was in the living room. Due to continuing headaches, she took a whole box of Extra Strength Goodie's with Coca Cola every day.

All of the kids in the neighborhood came to call her Mama, even some of the adults. She was a very good cook—Hmmmm! My taste buds still have lingering flavors of her scrumptious food.

She always told great stories. I mean the history-telling kind of stories and she acted a lot younger than her age. I loved my grandma.

This was the time when break dancing, football and "hide-and-go-get it" were the selection of hobbies and activities. There is always the memory of walking to Paso's to get the good meat, going across the street to the House of Prayer to get the free watermelon, and also going on 10th Street to the "icy lady's" house--now that I think about it, the house was disgustingly dirty.

I went along with my Uncle Kenny to build a rabbit trap one day. We rode our bikes down to 12th Street, positioning the homemade contraption in the woods hoping to trap a rabbit.

We left the trap for a few days, coming back every day to disappointment. Until one day when we came expecting to be disheartened yet again and there was a noise coming from within the wooden box.

We just stared at each other in amazement and smiled, looking like two guys that had just discovered precious water or struck gold.

Together, we lifted the box up on the front basket of Kenny's bicycle---it seemed very heavy for a rabbit. With great excitement and hearts racing we rode our bicycles home as fast as possible, yelling as we got closer, wanting everyone to see what we had caught. We gathered the Morrison Boys, the seven people that lived in my grandmother's house. We even invited the neighborhood drunk, Junky—who, by the way, could sing.

Uncle Kenny and I were both scared, but pretended not to be. Being typical boys, we did not want to admit to any weaknesses. We prepared to show off our prized catch. I was to open it and Kenny prepared his pellet gun---having it ready just in case it was not a friendly rabbit.

"Cupid draw back your bow and let your arrow flow straight to my lover's heart…for me," sang Junky, the drunk.

I opened the box, and to all of our shock and surprise, it was not a rabbit in the box.

OMG---it was a sharp-toothed possum---Yes, I said, POSSUM.

All of a sudden there was a bull stampede out of my grandmother's backyard, everyone screaming and running for dear life.

Lucky for us, the drunk wasn't afraid of it and was able to retrieve it and return it to the box. We took it to one of the neighbor's who knew what to do with it.

This incident has been talked about among the family for over 25 years.

Chapter 13

Hiding in plain sight

We constantly moved every few months---from my grandmother's to Piedmont Courts with my cousin Betty Jean, and finally back to North Charlotte, off the Plaza, on Duncan Avenue. It was a blue house on the corner, right behind the Pharmacy Drug Store.

The blue house consisted of two bedrooms, one bathroom, and squeaky floors. But it was a relief, the cessation of continuous moving. It had a nice size backyard with no grass because the last tenants prevented the grass from growing by parking cars on it.

We had a German Shepherd that we named Peanut. He was kept chained to a tree on the side of the house---I know what you are thinking, but that's the way it was back then.

I was at Hawthorne Middle School during this time and learning the ups and downs of being a teenager. For some reason I seemed to have a period of loneliness and a lack of concentration, not fully focusing.

I was too busy realizing that we were poor, which made me feel out of place, like I didn't belong. I felt not worthy of associating with anyone. All these thoughts stemmed from being poor.

There were all these little "clicks" in middle school and I didn't seem to know where to stand simply because I liked everyone. I wasn't smart in school, just your everyday average kid doing enough to get by, and for some reason I never liked reading in front of the class.

Perhaps it was because I had a problem with talking fast, composing my words and assembling my sentences. Every time I think about it, it makes me upset because when I talked slow at home, I spoke very well. Not to mention the fact that I had bad eyes that acted up just at the wrong moments---when they were not meant to.

And then there were the girls. I didn't really look or oogle at girls---not that I didn't like them---it was just the fear of being rejected. I must have been a very good actor because I don't think anyone knew I was so scared.

Being poor makes you desire things you can't afford, like better lunches and desserts purchased at school. Cake didn't come with the free lunch of square pizza, fries and whole milk. That didn't happen.

The clothes I did get were only at the beginning of the school year and had to be rotated with my brother Marvin and taken off after school.

I was so in awe of the kids wearing the "alligator shirts," Members Only jackets, and the Jordace jeans. We got a lot of our clothes from The Famous Mart on Independence Blvd. They had irregular clothes for cheaper than the normal price---the ones with the thread lines overlapping, buttons missing, and maybe the color just wasn't right or slightly faded.

But I was just glad to have those little possessions knowing my parents did the best they could to provide for us. There were the occasional times of coming home to no lights, water, and a number of times the sheriff's papers on the door for rent in arrears.

As a teenager, I would escape these issues by going skating on Sunday nights at Kate's Skating Rink on Central Avenue. I would try to forget there were problems to deal with at home or ignore they were happening.

The skating rink is where I would see Stacy Davidson. She was very tall, dark skinned, and had a nice big smile. She had an easy demeanor, dressed nicely and always looked very smart.

One night I was beside her and she spoke to me. I was in shock, not just because she spoke, but the fact that she knew my name or that I ever existed. We began talking about where we both lived and to my surprise she lived on Pinckney Avenue. I knew this street very well because my mom had worked at the school on the same road.

Pinckney Avenue was just four streets over from Duncan Avenue. Stacy was a little younger than me and attended Eastway Middle School. Soon, we spent many long nights on the phone—"You hang up," "No, you hang up,"--and falling asleep a few times. We were boyfriend and girlfriend.

Her life was a little different than mine. Her mother worked at the bank and her dad was a self-employed electrician who drove a Pontiac Firebird--sweet ride--with T-tops in it, blue with a large bird on the hood, and white letter tires. I was going to get me one of those cars one day. To me, Stacy was rich and it always bugged me not being able to buy her anything or just even invite her over to dinner, not knowing if we had enough for just us.

"Does it bug you that I am poor?" I would ask her.

"You are not poor," she would say, "you live in a house. Right? You have clothes on your back. Right? And you eat every night. Right?"

The answer to all her questions was Yes. I guess right then I realized not all people will judge you on what you have or don't have. And she never cared if I wasn't able to buy her things. She just wanted to be with me.

She taught me a lesson: she made me learn to accept and be blessed with what I have, to not dwell on what I don't have.

Most importantly, Stacy made me realize that you don't need to buy love.

Chapter 14

Garinger High School

I was finally over the "candy girl" issue. Now that all was well, I was happy. My eyes had improved immensely, and I was head over heels in love. So heading to high school was very exciting, and I looked forward to meeting new people.

I was in a homeroom full of diverse people, including Cedric Burton, who sat right behind me. Cedric was a black guy who played football. In front of me was Tawanta Allen—a very nice girl—whose race I never knew, but she looked a little Indian and had very pretty hair.

And then there was Paige Smith---oh boy! Paige was a pretty girl, very friendly, and had the prettiest smile in the world. I had a crush on her all three years of high school. Later in life, I would name one of my daughters Madison Paige Barnett. However,

I did not forget the fact, I had a girlfriend---so I never said a word.

High school just made my lack of money even that much clearer. And, it was at that point I decided that I would figure out a way to make money. The candy man was born. My new hustle would be to buy candy at the Pharmacy Drug Store for one price and resell it at school for another price.

Lollipops bought for 10 cents would sell for 25 cents, Now & Later's bought for 10 cents would sell for 20 and M&M's bought for 25 cents would sell for 50. I was in business and making good money. I think maybe I even sold a few candies to the teachers.

I had become really good friends with Cedric and we added Chris Jones to the mix, which was good and bad. Chris was a funny-talking kid who always wanted to tell jokes which were never really funny. It was just the way he talked that made it sound funny.

For some odd reason Chris seemed to always pay me to do his homework. I never knew why, because I wasn't very smart. But, for some reason, he always passed or was moved on to the next grade.

Cedric, the jock, never really got the jokes, but he would just smile out of politeness. Then he would make eye contact with me, as if to say "Is he serious?"

Garinger was the place to be back then. Auto Shop class, Radio-TV broadcasting and Graphic Arts were my favorite classes. I always looked forward to lunch time when we would leave school and go to McDonald's on North Tyron Street.

We all knew very well that we were not supposed to leave school grounds, but we went regardless, and always managed to sneak back into school grounds without getting caught. This was the hardest part, because there were a few teachers who made it their job to try and catch you.

Then there were the basketball games, football, and proms that we looked forward to each year. We had very pretty girls at Garinger: Charlotte, Carla, Nina, Paige, Beverly, and Shannon just to name a few.

All of the boys were cool and got along most of the time. There was Pervis, Darrel, Tony, Cool Rob and Carey--just a few who were cool with me. Then the couples that were inseparable: Charlotte and Pervis, Nina and Jr., and of course, Pricilla and Russell—"The Gold Standard," I called them.

Pricilla a very pretty girl with a big smile, and was always nice and polite to everyone. Russell was very tall, dark skinned guy who was cool and easy going. They were a perfect fit—as I finished this book, they had celebrated their 21 year anniversary.

The little North Charlotte crew--- Nicole-dimples, Gironda(birdie),Beverly-who I always thought was a cutie, Dee and Nina, the fighter--I never saw a girl or guy she wouldn't fight. They had a pretty solid bond because they had all been friends since middle school.

We even had a guy that ran for Carousel Queen in 1986--Queen Nick they called him. He didn't win, but we were on the news, so that was pretty cool.

One day I was driving my Uncle Oscar's car to school and some of the guys asked me if I wanted to go with them over to Independence High School to just hang out.

These boys were the tough guys at school, and I wanted to fit in, so I agreed and even told them I drove to school that day. Why did I have to open my big mouth? Little did I know that the real reason they wanted to go over to the school was to settle a weekend fight.

We drove to the school and walked the halls as if we were enrolled students there. I saw my cousin, Wanda Jackson, so we talked for few minutes and then I headed back to the parking lot with the guys.

I was thinking to myself, "Since we didn't see the guys they were looking for, we are leaving."

But, that didn't happen.

We noticed two white guys walking towards their car in the parking lot. One of the boys with us decided he was going to take their chain, and that's exactly what he did.

He walked up to them without fear and just pulled it off the guy's neck. Then we pretty much ran to the car and sped off. I wanted to ask why he did that, but I just sat quietly trying not to look uncool. They talked about the "snatch and run" incident as if it was no big deal while we drove back to Garinger.

We got caught coming back in school, so detention was the next stop. We never thought about the fact maybe someone got the tag number on the car. Well, they did, and the police went to my uncle's house. He, in return, told them his nephew had borrowed his car.

The police came to the school and I was called to the office and immediately told that I was in trouble. All of our names were on the detention list, the same number of boys that were rumored to have been at Independence and on the same date we had be caught together coming back on campus so it was very easy to figure out who did it.

These boys were responsible for several chain robberies, so it was very easy for the police to put two and two together. We were suspended for six months, and sent to Street Academy, a school for troubled youths.

I have to tell you, I was the only one that participated in Street Academy. I guess the other guys were too cool for school at that point, and they all dropped out. I intended to finish school. I enjoyed school thoroughly, so I went.

I knew that I needed to concentrate on what I had to, in order to get back to normal. And that's what I did. I learned a valuable lesson: rebelling just to be down with the tough guys, and trying to fit in with the wrong crowd spells TROUBLE.

I told myself, "I'm just going to be myself and if that isn't good enough—Oh, well."

After six months I finished my time at the Street Academy, did some soul searching, and talked with my uncle Oscar. He wisely advised me to always be a leader not a follower.

I had one thing on my mind after this: my first priority was getting my life back on track. The plan was to finish high school, go into the Marines as a military policeman--just because I thought the uniforms were cool. Then I would go to college with the money earned from the Marines.

That was the original plan!

Chapter 15

The dealership and the promise

Half way through my 11th grade year, I got a job at Western Sizzlin Streak House on Independence Blvd. I commenced as a dishwasher. My co-worker was a guy name Kevin Seabrooks. He was a boxer, training to fight for IBF World Championship. He was very sure of himself.

I knew him because he lived in my neighborhood and my Aunt Peaches Jackson and he were friends. I always believed in him and admired his drive and determination. He trained like no other, jogged before work, shadowboxed on lunch breaks, and he would jog home after long rigorous nights of washing dishes.

I knew if there was something I wanted to achieve, I had to be just like he was about his goal: FOCUSED!

Kevin went on, to not only become IBF World Champion 1987, but also USBA Champion, US Olympic Trials Bronze Medalist, and ESPN fighter of the decade. At the time my goal was not as big as his, but I wanted a car—and not just any car. I wanted a Mustang.

I would ride the No. 2 bus past my job up to Town & Country Ford for motivation and to admire the cars. Then I would happily walk back down the street to work.

I began saving money, but it was taking me forever to save enough for a down payment. There were always things I needed and also, I had to give my Aunt Carolyn Jackson rent money because I had moved into the Idlewild Apartments with her by then.

After about eight months, I had what I felt was a good down payment of $1500. It was few weeks before my senior year had started, so it would be great to have a car for my senior year. I went to Town & Country Ford one Friday thinking, "I'm going to get my car."

I arrived at the dealership, very excited about the vast variety of car colors and couldn't make up my mind which one I wanted: black with tan seats, red with chrome wheels or blue with a sunroof.

I noticed that no one had approached me to offer any assistance, so I walked inside and asked if someone could help me look for a car. The salesman looked at me with distaste. He had already formed an opinion based on my looks, and I sensed he was thinking I was wasting his time.

"Can I help you out with something young man?" he asked me, unenthusiastically. I informed him, that I was very interested in buying a car.

"When will you have a down payment?" he said.

"I have it now," I said proudly.

Immediately his eyes lit up and his attitude changed. Suddenly, he was all over me like a rash with, "Mr. Barnett this," or "Mr. Barnett that."

I test drove the red Mustang and I loved it. We got back to the dealership, signed the paperwork, and they had it washed for me. But, then there was a problem.

"You need a co-signer," the manager said, "because you have never had credit."

"Let's go see my Uncle Oscar Agurs," I said.

I was sure he could help me solve this problem. I drove the car to his house and told him of my plan and that I needed his help. He looked over the paper work and frowned. Then he pulled me to the side and advised me it was not a good deal.

"Wait until morning," he said, "and I will go with you to find a car."

The next day my uncle told me to meet him at City Chevrolet. I got there and my uncle was already talking to a salesman.

Confused, I thought to myself, "there are no Mustangs here!"

I was shown a Chevette—a small and not very fascinating car, without a sunroof, and it wasn't very fast.

I never liked it, but out of respect for my uncle, I held my comments to myself because I figured Oscar knew what I needed. Maybe he felt a Mustang was too fast for me, or, perhaps, it was not a good first car.

I had to wait until Monday to get insurance, so I couldn't take the car that day. I just sat miserably in it for few more minutes.

Then I looked over at the Beck Mercedes Dealership. I made a mental note to myself, "I will never buy car I don't like again, regardless of any influence." I also promised myself that one day, before I turned 35, I would walk in there and buy a car.

.... And I did—but that's another story.

Chapter 16

The summer of 1987

The last few weeks of school were a combination of good and bad, happy and sad. This was because you were completing the first part of your schooling, but, at the same time, you were leaving some good friends, making career choices and everyone was going in their chosen paths, towards the next chapter of their lives.

We finished high school on June 5,1987, graduating at the Charlotte Coliseum on Independence Blvd. My whole family came to support me and see me graduate from school.

No one in my family had graduated in the traditional way since my Aunt Patricia ten years before, so it felt great to have so much family beaming with pride and showing love and support.

I received some gifts, congratulations, and a lot of hugs. My personal favorite gift was the $200 that my Uncle James gave me to buy some chrome wheels for the Chevette. Back then, those were rims of choice and I had to have them.

The next morning, I purchased the wheels, new seat covers and, naturally, the dice to hang off the mirror. I was so proud of that car after getting use to it and the best part is, it was all mine. I washed it every three days, keeping it sparkling and glistening in the sun. I also kept those tree air freshener's in heavy rotation. Not many people my age had a car in my neighborhood, so I was beaming with joy and was very proud of that car.

I was pretty content with my overall plans, my girlfriend, and my life to this point. I spent the first half of the summer working and hanging out with Stacy. I also had two good friends, Darrin Miller and Andrew Smith. I would hang out with them when I wasn't with Stacey.

The guys and I would often hang out at Tryon Mall Movie Theater on the weekends. We would always see these two sisters, Bippy and Shan House, and their cousin, Money. We all became good friends with the girls and started hanging out together a lot.

This was recipe for disaster because I had a girlfriend and I knew this could go all wrong, but I continued to hang out with them. I think the plan was for Shan and me to get together, but for some reason Bippy and I always ended up talking to each other.

Before you know it, we ended up kissing one night. This would be the first of many times I would cheat and I was spending less time with Stacy. So you see, Stacy was a very safe choice, pretty, and overall a nice girlfriend. But she was spending too much time with her parents and they didn't let her go out much.

In comparison to Stacy was Bippy who could go anywhere. She was the kind of girl edging towards The Danger Zone and that excited me. She lived with her aunt and throughout the duration of Bippy and Shan's stay, her aunt was drinking a lot, and leaving the girls with there big sister Betty to tend them. That meant the girls had their freedom and pretty much did as they pleased, even allowing me to stay overnight.

So now I was faced with a problem: how would I end it with Stacy? Could I be a player and keep them both?

One day I was told Stacy was at the swimming pool hanging out with some guys we both knew. Now I knew her well enough to know she wasn't that kind of girl, but I used this opportunity to break up with her.

I caused a big fight about her being around them, pretending like I was very hurt and upset. Stacy was looking at me like, "What are you talking about?"

"I don't want a girlfriend that hang out and flirt with other guys," I said, "and I am breaking up with you."

I used "reverse psychology" on her, taking my guilt about cheating and put it on her. For years, she would always tell me that I left her to be with Bippy, but I denied it.

One day out of the blue, Darrin said he knew a way for us to make some real money.

"I got a job," I said.

"No," he said, "I mean a lot of money."

So Andrew and I waited to hear this get rich money plan Darrin seemed to have figured out.

"We can take $200," he said, "and turn it into $1200 in just few days."

Andrew and I looked at it each other like, "OK, but what's the catch?"

"We can buy some drugs and resell them," he said.

"No way," I said, "Are you crazy?"

Darrin went on to explain how the procedure works--it was easy and we could do it a few times before we just stopped.

After thinking about it and Darrin making it seem like a breeze, I said, “OK, what we need to do?”

“We just need $200,” he said, “and we’re on our way.”

“Well,” I said, “I have $200 in my savings account that we can use to get started.”

I gave him the money, and he left. A little while later he came back with this white powder which he pointed out was cocaine. He had it all bagged up and separated in little plastic bags with ties on them.

He handed me $400 worth, Andrew $400 worth and he kept $400 worth for himself.

“Well,” I said, “where we are going to sell it at?”

The plan was I would sell on Belmont Avenue in north Charlotte, Andrew in Piedmont Courts, and Darrin would go to Earle Village.

So we headed off in our separate directions, calling ourselves drug dealers. I didn’t see them anymore that week. I sold all I had and was waiting to hear from both guys.

When I finally saw Darrin, he said that he had lost his share of it. I instantly knew it was a lie because I had precisely heard he was using drugs himself. Then he told me that Andrew had been over in Wilmore playing spin the barrel with a 357 magnum and had killed someone. He was in jail for murder.

I was totally surprised at this because Andrew was always quiet. I never would have believed him to be the type to play with a gun--but then again, who is?

I headed home to figure out what I would do next. I decided that I would continue selling drugs until I signed into the Marines in August--seemed simple enough at the time.

Little did I know the money would keep rolling in and fast. In less than a month I had made over $10,000. because I would sell all day and half the night, buying over and over. It was just too easy. I was very organized, packaging the product, keeping track of how much I made by writing it down in "telephone form" or putting it in "address formation."

I kept telling myself, "I'm stopping in one more week." But, August came and went. By September, I had made what some people make in a year on a good job. It became addictive and the whole rush of knowing you are trying to outsmart the police was exciting.

At this point the Marines weren't even in the plans anymore, and I had rented an apartment and brought two more cars. The only bad news was, most people, including the police, knew what I was doing by now and I was working less hours. I mean, by now, I could almost buy my own restaurant.

My attitude toward going to work for $240 week did not make sense when I could make that in a few minutes. But, I knew I had to cover myself.

I could pretty much afford anything I wanted and Bippy would be walking around in high school with $500 in her pocket. We were living the high life.

This was just the beginning of something bigger and better. Over the next few months I would proceed to make on an average of 10-15 thousand dollars a month. The idea of working was not in my future.

I would think, “It takes one whole hour to make $5.50?” The thought of working my butt off to make $5.50 an hour didn’t appeal to me one little bit at all. I was making so much money, I would give away $100-$200 a day to the neighborhood kids, so you know I wasn’t going to work all day for $40-$50.

I had completely forgotten about any plans because the money was coming in too easily. At the time I assumed this could last forever because I kept a low profile and I didn’t trust anyone enough to let them get close to me---not even Bippy.

Chapter 17

The rise to power

By 1989, I had made so much money that I could do and buy pretty much anything and everything I wanted. The police were very upset about this and made it their personal goal to catch me. Most of the time, they came away frustrated because I never left anything unsecured while building my Empire.

I was a beast when it came to details of the operation. It was so tight at this point, I had five guys working under me and they had four to five under them who never came in contact with me. I didn't really know who they were and I didn't care about making friends with any of them. This was business, and there's no room or time for friends or sloppy operations. I was 19 years old and had purchased a house, a four-bay auto repair shop, and six cars.

My favorite car was my white-on-white Mercedes with the white wheels. I had seen a car Morris Day drove in the movie Purple Rain and I wanted the same car, so I went out and got it from the Beck Dealership...Wink.

I added new seats, radio, and a phone in the car. Try to remember this car was never seen in the ghetto. I was in total control and was high maintenance. I was well-liked in neighborhoods where I made my money, by making a life promise to always give back to the community. It made me feel better because I was dividing so many lives and supporting their addictions to gain my wealth and my place in history.

I was the bad guy, but everyone liked me because under the shield of toughness, was still Spencer. I cared about people. But, the more money I made, the more problems arose.

Anytime you start earning so much money, the jealously will slowly surface out of people and I did notice it. This made me become even more guarded, suspicious to the point that when I would go out, I didn't talk much. I always had three to four guys around me, watching my back, and I had them watching each other. I trusted no one.

By now I was making 40k on a slow month and the police were on high alert for me. They even had a program called Operation Silent Night with my picture and other hustlers' pictures on the Christmas tree at the police station.

I had respect for the police and they for me, but I was a hustler and it was their job to catch me. I was truly blessed because I had the people on my side in the neighborhoods: North Charlotte, Piedmont Court's, Earle Village, and in most other neighborhoods I went to, the people looked out for me.

Being so wealthy also had its perks, like attracting attention from the ladies. I had girlfriends in every neighborhood and some even lived in the same neighborhoods. They didn't care about the others as long as I took care of a bill, hairdo, or some other money issues they would encounter. That's just the way it was back then.

I was a ghetto celebrity. I had never really looked at myself as a good looking guy, so I knew it was about the money, which was OK with me because I wasn't going to give any more than I wanted to give them. I guess, by now, you see I played the game well.

You can't out play a player, out con a con-man, and I was competent---but, really, I was clever at it. There were many mutual hustlers around the city but, among the majority, there was respect because everyone had their own space.

Don't get me wrong there were still many issues, conflicts and even gun-play at times. But most of the hustlers wanted money more than being a gangster, and we had our hands full just trying to stay a step ahead of the police and their technology.

The police were getting better and would be out trying to catch a hustler with night vision goggles, dogs, and the occasional planted crack heads. It got to the point where they were even catching people and letting them go in exchange for them setting others up. This made me become even more guarded.

One night the guys and I drove out to my Uncle James' club, The Apollo, in North Charlotte on Pegram Street. We usually took three cars as a precaution; that way we would have the right amount of guys in case there was trouble.

We arrived at the club and, for some reason, my intuition was sensing very bad vibes. I just couldn't relax. I was watching everyone like a hawk from my table. Every movement made me nervous and jumpy. I didn't really drink, but had a gin and orange juice just to relax my nerves. That way I could still keep my eyes on everyone.

I remember thinking at the time, "I need to find a guy to be my eyes, someone I can trust to watch everyone and everything around me so that I can go out and relax."

I had noticed this young guy, about 17 years old, who would always bug me about wanting to work with me. I didn't want any of the guys already working for me to be my eyes, nor did I want an old gangster, because they were too ambitious and would try to obliterate me, to take over.

I thought, "This kid has potential."

I used to call him The Player because he was a star football player in high school. I used to tell him when he completed school, I would think about him working for me, hoping he would forget about it and end up playing football in college or for the pros.

But now I needed him and I knew that he would be delighted to accept and would do his utmost to impress me---so happy that he wouldn't want to let me down.

Once he graduated high school, he approached me again. I stared at him sternly.

"Are you 100% sure this is what you want to do?" I asked him, "Because once you are in, there's no way out."

Instantly and without a moment of hesitation, he said. "Yes."

"Don't ever cross me," I warned him, "or you will regret it."

I took him under my wing for months, testing him along the way. I watched him closely when he wasn't aware I was watching. He was very scared at first, but as he watched me his self-esteem and confidence were built up day by day. Everyone knew he was soon to be my eyes and ears. I told him the key to it all was to be a businessman, not a gangster.

"Gangsters don't last long," I told him. "They are feared, not loved and people will love to see you fall."

Chapter 18

With money comes confidence

I was still with Bippy during my climb to the top of the food chain, but with money came more attention from the women. Previously, I was scared of girls or really lacked confidence with the opposite sex. Now I found it easy because they were so busy trying to keep me happy.

I didn't have to talk so much or worry about rejection and before I knew it, I perfected the best "talk game" there was. It didn't make much difference what I talked about—these women would willingly go along with it.

The women all knew Bippy was my main woman, living with me on The Ranch as we called my home out on Lawyers Road.

Beverly was a dark-skinned beauty queen. She had pretty long black hair and the smile of an angel. She was an only child who lived with her mother on

Siegle Avenue in a little apartment behind Fat's Store. She was about 18 years old and was in her last year of high school.

I really liked her because of the way she was raised and she was very mature for her age. I trusted her with more than most people. I could always count on her for anything and her mother really liked me, so that made it a lot easier. I knew if I wasn't hustling, she would make a great wife and I always felt she was too good for my life style, so I tried my hardest to shelter her and keep her away from the streets.

Then there was Lavinna. She was a nice sweet girl, about 19, with a one year-old son. She was a little more street-wise than Beverly, but didn't have a bad name in the streets. She was a little naive and I could get away with a lot with her, but I knew she really cared about me. She was a ride-or-die chick. I put her in an apartment and paid all the bills. I could leave money with her and not worry about it Because of the quantity of money I made, I needed more places to hide it. Her and her little posse of friends were cool Paps, Dee, and Danita.

Sweet was a girl that I had dated off and on over the years. She was very pretty with a great smile and a very hot body. She was 19, lived with her little sister and mother in Griertown on dead-end street. She always took care of herself and her little sister. Her mother was a drinker, for some time back then, so Sweet pretty much raised herself and her little sister.

Sweet was different from the other girls. I would give her money, but she would also hustle herself and was good at it. I was never really sure about her and I didn't trust her at times because she was capable of getting into stuff or involved with other guys. But that's how our relationship was, and it worked for us.

Next was Tokie. At 27, she was much older. I was just 20 at the time. Tokie was married to another local hustler. There was always the danger of being caught and having to deal with him, but she loved being with me.

Tokie was a very nice looking lady who had a very strong resemblance to Stacy Latisaw, the singer. She never asked me for anything, just loved to have sex every time we were together and she was good at it. She would always inform me what her husband was planning or what his next move was, therefore keeping me one step ahead of him.

And last, but not least, there was Toya, "The Cheerleader". She was fresh out of high school and green as a lime. She was by far the prettiest of them all and could pass off as Lisa Raye. She was very skinny, happy, and had a lot of energy.

I was out one Sunday with my Uncle Tony, driving around. We decided to go past the Bojangles on East Blvd. This was the place to be every Sunday--where everyone went for a cruise and to show off their cars.

Tony was driving my sports car and I was the passenger. We went into the parking lot and Toya was walking out of Bojangles. I spoke to her and asked her over to the car and we flirted for a few minutes. That's how she became my girlfriend a few weeks later.

All them knew of each other. They knew I dated other girls sometimes---but they never said much about the others, at least not to me.

Bippy had heard a lot of talk about me being with all these girls on the side and was jealous as she was pregnant with my first child. She gave me an ultimatum: marry her or she was leaving.

I simply replied OK. I didn't want to be married right then, but I knew I would marry her one day, so I just said OK.

A few days later, together with my mother, Aunt Carolyn and Bippy's cousin, Money, we drove down to the York Court House to seal our marriage. It didn't take long and we were finally married.

It didn't register well in my head that I was married because I cheated a week later with Tokie in my house on Woodlawn Road.

Bippy, who was supposed to be in school, came home and had her cousin and Aunt with her. They caught me with Tokie in the guest bedroom with my clothes off and, boy, it did not end well.

Although I was caught, I would still continue to see all of the girlfriends throughout the entire marriage. It has occurred to me that because of the unfortunate encounters that happened with Feet and Cookie when I was a kid, I never cared about how many women I slept with---whatever was said to me about having boundaries, respecting myself or respecting women fell on deaf ears.

I was ignorant, and I was in control. I would not let anyone control me, or let them tell me how to live my life. This was my lifestyle and it didn't matter who got hurt in the process. My attitude and lack of respect towards women were, in the end, due to my childhood trauma.

I was wrong.

Chapter 19

She looks like you

Bippy was days away from giving birth to the baby and we were ready. I was still young, but knew I could take care of the baby. We had already read the books, decorated the bedroom, and taken the Lamaze classes. I figured we had prepared as good as anyone.

I knew that I was going to give this baby any and everything she wanted---guess you could say we went little overboard on the clothes. I tried to spend more time at home during Bippy's last month and she was happy to have me around more.

"I hope you stop having all these women on the side," I remember her saying. "Let's just be a family."

I agreed with her and even tried it for few weeks, but I just loved the all of the attention and I had developed a very high sex drive, not sure if my childhood contributed to this or not, but I always wanted it.

Bippy was not always willing to give, especially considering she was nine months pregnant---it would lead to many fights. That would be my excuse for going out in the streets with these other women.

June 6, 1990, I was awakened by the howling of the neighbor's dog. I got up and went to the door to see why he was carrying on so bad. I was calling his name, but he just kept barking. I put my jacket on top of my PJs and walked over to the white lady's door thinking maybe she was asleep or just didn't hear her dog barking--after all, she was 81 years old.

I must have knocked on that door 20 minutes and still no answer. I looked down and noticed the door was cracked, so I push it open a little to call to her.

"Mrs. Carter," I called. "Mrs. Carter…" But still---nothing. I was a little worried now because she never went anywhere. She had stopped driving and would only leave if her daughter came by.

I went in still calling to her and as soon as I got in the door, there she was sitting in the chair.

I was thinking or hoping she was asleep. I called her name again. I walked over to her thinking, "Oh, my God, this lady might be dead."

I reached her chair and touched her on the shoulder. In that moment, I got a cold chill up my back---sure enough she was dead.

I just was in shock and just couldn't move. I pushed myself over to the phone after a few minutes and called the police and her daughter. It's very hard to tell someone their loved one has passed.

After the police and the ambulance arrived, I gave them my statement of what had happened and went back into my house. I didn't even wake Bippy to tell her what had just transpired. I didn't want to start her day off with that news; she was already in an odd state of mind. I just got dressed and went to meet the guys.

At the spot, we headed out for the day as we had always done. I was feeling funny all day considering I had found my neighbor dead. I just wasn't in mood for doing much, so I had the guys drop me off at Beverly's house—We were no longer in a relationship, but I could always go there when I wanted to get away.

I fell asleep for close to four hours.

When I woke up, my pager—yes, pager---was full of numbers, most of them from Bippy.

"Why did you let me sleep so long?" I asked Beverly.

"You seemed like you was tired," she said.

I jumped up and called the phone in the Mercedes. The Player answered it, I told him to pick me up. Soon as he got there, I got in the car and called Bippy because I couldn't call her from Beverly's landline.

All could make out in-between Bippy's curse words was something about my being at Beverly's house. I figured it must be the girl across the parking lot at Beverly's. She didn't care for me much because at one time she liked me and I never looked at her. She always made it a point to rat me out.

I headed to the house to calm Bippy down. I arrived to her sitting on the side porch looking like she could choke me death---right now.

She started yelling at me about all the promises I had made about this and that, this girl, that girl. In between all of that, she asked why I didn't tell her the neighbor died.

I couldn't say much because I was wrong, so I did what I had always done, saying, "I don't have time for this," and went to my car and pulled off.

About ten minutes later she called and said her water had broken. I was thinking she was lying just to get me to come back home. I called my mother.

"Do you think Bippy is lying?" I asked. "I don't remember anything about water breaking in class."

"Boy," my mother said, "if you don't get your butt back to that house and get her to the hospital, you going to have to deal with me."

I turned around and went back to the house. Bippy was sitting at the kitchen table and the floor was wet.

"Are you OK?" I asked. She nodded.

"Grab suitcase by the front door," she said.

I helped her up, guided her out the side door to the Dodge Caravan that I had purchased for the baby and we headed to the hospital.

I was speeding, so, of course, the police pulled me over.

"My wife's in labor," I yelled out the window back to his police car as he got out.

"Follow me," he said and jumped back in his car.

I must admit it felt weird to have the police helping me.

"Good luck," the policeman said when we made it to the hospital.

"Thank you," I said.

While Bippy was getting checked in, they were asking a million questions while she was in pain.

"Can't you guys do all of that later?" I said.

"Sir," the desk lady said, "we need this information so we can make sure everything goes well."

I was thinking, "How can something go wrong?"

I started praying, saying "God, I know I have not talked to You in a while, but I'm asking You to watch over Bippy and the baby, so that they will be OK."

You see we forget God until we need something from Him. I had clearly forgotten Him, thinking I was doing it all on my own. I think it was the other people's prayers that kept me safe.

Soon we were in the operating room and there were people everywhere hooking up machines and saying all these words that I didn't understand or care to know.

I just wanted the baby out and both of them to be OK afterwards. About four more hours of screaming, waiting, and more screaming, the baby is deciding she will take her own sweet time to make her appearance, so there was more waiting.

About 30 minutes later, the baby was low and ready to come out. With Bippy digging into my arm, calling me everything but the Son of God and pushing, the baby came out. I think we all gave sigh of relief.

When the medical staff had finished checking everything on the baby, they wrapped her up good and with a few instructions, they handed her back to Bippy.

I just stared at the baby, thinking, "Wow …."

We had already decided her name would be Mercedes Simone Barnett. She was so beautiful and little. It was at that moment we were a family and nothing else mattered.

God had taken one of His children and replaced her with another one on earth. What a crazy day.

Now I was a dad.

The nurse turned to me with a big smile.

"She looks like you," she said.

She looks like you!

Chapter 20

$13,890.00

In 1992, I was at my peak and I was untouchable. I was raking in so much money I was having difficulties hiding it. I let my guard down and I did things I wouldn't normally do, like taking a chance by leaving money with different women and friends, hoping they would stay loyal and not steal from me.

Sometimes I would just go and buy a car or something I didn't need just to use the money up. Like I said before, I was real organized and kept track of all the money I had made up until this point, even money that was spent. I was still writing it down in codes or as phone numbers, on the walls, inside of books and even behind insulations in the walls.

I remember one day I was out making my rounds, nothing out of the ordinary. I met up with one of the main bosses and he had some money for me secured in a little box.

"It's a little short," he said. "I will get you the rest in a few hours."

"How short is it?" I said. "Do I need to count it?"

"No," he said, "it's $13,890. I owe you $1,110 to make it $15,000."

"OK," I said. "Take the rest and buy your kids something nice from Uncle Doc." Doc was the nickname I had been tagged with.

I took that box to this girl, Lisa, I knew. I would hang out with her from time to time and asked her to keep the box for me. She lived on Reddman Road near the carwash in an apartment on the hill.

After having relations with her, I headed back out, telling her I would come back later. She and I knew that I wouldn't be back that night, but that's how it was.

I went to Earle Village to talk with my grandmother and have some of her good soup--you know the kind that makes you lean over to the side afterwards!

"I want to talk to you about something," she said.

"OK, Mama," I said. "Let's go outside on the park bench."

We went outside. I saw a few people standing around talking, the crazy neighborhood drunk was in full singing mood and DeVondia Roseburough and her little sister were sitting on their back wall.

"Hi, Spencer Barnett." It was DeVondia, yelling out my government name. By now, everyone called me Doc. DeVondia was the only person that I was OK with calling me my real name. I guess it was just the way she said it--all in one breath.

We reached the park benches and my grandmother began to talk to me about how proud she was of me for always doing things for the kids and the community. Don't get me wrong, she didn't want me selling drugs, but she knew it was part of my life.

"Don't lose track of God," she said, "and of yourself because you will have a heavy price to pay. Keep God with you at all times, because I love you and it worries me sometimes when I don't see you for a few days."

I guess in the last three to four years I had neglected The Almighty and had not attended church or prayed much.

"I can't tell you what to do," she said, "but you need to think about your life passed this time and your wife and your daughter."

"OK, Mama, I will," I said and walked her back to her door. I headed back to the cars where the guys had been waiting.

"You guys take the other cars," I said to them, "and I'll meet up with you later."

They looked at me very oddly because I never drove myself much or went many places alone.

"Just do it," I said.

I got a call as I was driving down Independence Blvd. heading to The Ranch. It was Lisa. She said her ex-boyfriend had been by when I was there earlier and saw my car outside and now he keeps knocking on the door and driving around the parking lot.

I went by her place but he was nowhere in sight when I got there.

"I'm going to my mother's house for the night," she said. "You might want to take your money because he has a key still." She didn't know if he would come inside while she was away.

I got the box and watched her drive off. I waited around for a few more minutes just to see if her ex would drive by again but he never did. I headed home.

I arrived at The Ranch, went inside and got some pizza out of the refrigerator. I didn't know how old it was because I had not been there in three days and Bippy was not home.

I went downstairs to the basement to get my papers from behind the dryer and I looked at them. I added the $13,890 to the total already calculated. I was totally surprised to see how much it was that I had made from 1987-1992. Let's just say I hit the seven figures family.

I remember thinking to myself, "There's no need to write down anything ever again."

I took all my papers and other things I had calculated on and burned them in the fireplace. I walked over to the back door and walked out on the deck, took a seat and absorbed it all in. To this day, I hadn't ever told anyone how much money I had made.

Stage 3:

When I became a man:
I gave up childish ways…

Chapter 21

The phone Call

I knew that I had a great life. I was young, rich, and had a great family. But I knew my hustler's life would not end well, because they never did.

A hustler would go to jail, get on his own drugs, or end up dead. I remember always thinking that I wouldn't live to see 40. I mean, I would have loved to live this way forever, but knew that would not be possible.

I knew soon or later someone would turn on me. I noticed the difference in people. I had let many people go on bad terms.

One day, I was leaving my grandmother's house with The Cheerleader, heading to my house to change clothes. At this point Bippy and I no longer were together.

I saw my little cousin, Charles Jackson, walking down near Piedmont Courts under the bridge. I pulled over.

"Where you going?" I said.

"To Uncle James' club," he said, "to watch the Super Bowl."

"OK," I said, "I'm heading to my house…I will be there later."

I pulled off, but stopped a few feet away.

"You want a ride over there?" I said.

"Sure."

I took him to the club and headed to my house.

The Cheerleader and I were both little tired, so we decided to take a nap. Our plan was to go over to the club to watch the game. But we overslept and missed the game.

I sat up on the side of the bed and looked at my pager; it was full of numbers, but that was not out of the normal.

I noticed my Uncle Oscar's number.

I thought, "What would he be doing calling me at 12.13AM."

Uncle Oscar was a square who went to bed at 9:00PM and never called me much. I called him back.

“Charles has been shot at the club and is in hospital,” he said.

I said many curse words, forgetting that Uncle Oscar was a preacher.

I got dressed and sped down Independence Blvd. I was near the Charlotte Coliseum when my phone in the car rang. It was Uncle Oscar saying that Charles had passed away.

My heart just dropped. I had to pull over on the shoulder under the bridge. I couldn’t believe my little cousin was dead.

When I looked up, the first thing that popped into my head was, “Someone is going to pay.” I knew full well this wasn’t the answer, but it made sense at the time.

I called The Player, to say meet me, but they were already at my grandmother’s house waiting on me.

Outside, I gave them a nod to hold on a minute and went into my grandmother’s apartment where the family was gathered. I had one question.

“Who did it?” I asked.

Everyone tried to calm me down, but it wasn’t working, so I headed out the door. The family knew there would be trouble because there were about six guys waiting on me.

My grandmother followed me outside and pulled me to the side.

"Pray, baby," she said. "That's what we have to do for them."

"OK, Mama," I said. "I'm going to head home and wait until tomorrow for it to all get worked out."

"Love you, baby," she said, but she knew I was lying.

"Love you, too, Mama," I said.

We headed out on Caldwell Street and went to North Charlotte with one thing on our minds---find whoever killed Charles. God has a funny way of protecting us from ourselves, sometimes, because we didn't cross paths with anyone that night.

The next day the shooter turned himself in to the police. I don't know what I was thinking the night before. I mean, why would I want to put another mother through what my Aunt Charlie was dealing with?

Chapter 22

The Set Up And Downfall

I knew this was the beginning of a lot of trouble. I lost all interest in hustling. Bippy began to enjoy her own affairs, but were already separated. I wasn't being my normal self. And I wasn't the only one---after my cousin's death, several family members turned to drugs or drinking.

I was in a very different space and mind frame. I was doing things that I wouldn't normally do and trusting people to do things when I should have known better.

The only thing I was happy about was the fact that, due to a lot of missing evidence at his retrial, Andrew was out. Right on the spot I made him my "go to" guy.

The other guys never like the idea of Andrew just coming in, ranking so high, when they had put in years. But, Andrew was my boy.

He seemed a bit strange when he was released, but I didn't read too much into it during that time. In the beginning he was always around asking many questions and happy he could buy whatever he wanted.

But, then his behavior changed. He would disappear for days at a time and was asking more and more questions about my source and what it was costing me.

I overlooked all this and assumed he wanted to learn the business or even go out on his own soon.

Not really wanting to hustle anymore and after trying many times to quite, "

I got to get out of this life soon," I said. To myself.

I called the guys up one Saturday, had them meet me over at my shop on South Tyron Street---near Tape City---and informed them that I was done with the hustling business.

"If you need money to get going, let me know, because I was going to be working at my shop and letting this life go," I said.

Many of them were surprised and very confused.

"What do we do now?" some of them asked.

"You live," I said. "You can't base your life around me."

This new life went fine for two months until a good buddy of mine got a big load and wanted me to help him unload it. He was giving me a very good spread, so I agreed to help him.

"I'll help you dump it," I said, "then I'm back to what I'm doing here." Big mistake!

I got most of it gone and was down to last few ounces, when I was in the office at the shop and Andrew came in the door.

"What's up man?" I said. I had not seen him lately; I knew he was making moves on his own.

"Just been hustling," he said, "but I don't have anything right now. Do you have anything? I can pay. I don't need a front or anything."

I hesitated for one minute.

"Yes, man," I said, "I'll look out for you." I walked him into the back of the shop where we had old Ford Escort at the back corner and lifted the hatchback up and gave him one ounce.

"How much I owe you?" he said.

"Take it," I said. "Pay me later, man."

"Thank you, man," he said. "I got to get out of here and go make this happen.

"OK, be safe," I said.

He left the shop and I returned to my office to finish the Hang Man game. About ten minutes later, when I was in the middle of playing on the computer, six plain clothes police walked into the shop showing their badges.

"Go to the front of the shop," they said.

Standing there, I knew some of the faces of the officers because they had being trying to catch me for years. After searching everyone, they went straight to the Ford Escort and found the drugs.

All eight people were going to jail, they said, because they didn't find the drugs on anyone. The car was just an old one we had gotten from the junk yard for parts, so they really couldn't point it back to owner of car. I knew they wanted me and the drugs were mine.

"It's mine," I said. "No reason to take the other guys. They had no knowledge of it being there."

The police looked at each other. Their looks seemed to say, "Did you hear that?" One of the officers pulled me to the side.

"Are you sure this is what you want to say?" he said.

"Yes," I said.

After telling the other guys they were lucky, the police let them up off the floor and walked me to the unmarked Ford Mustangs. I turned to my Uncle Kenny.

"Call my mother," I said.

“You’re a stand-up guy, nephew,” he said, nodding.

I was finally riding in a Mustang.

“Is it good on gas?” I asked the police. They seemed surprised at my asking, since I had just gotten busted.

You see, there were a few things that I knew and they didn’t. I knew Andrew set me up---but that didn’t matter. I knew that I would be out in few hours and I knew that I had just gotten my way out of the drug game that day.

I never really had an exit plan or ever stuck to quitting---so I was just fine.

Chapter 23

Spencer vs. Spencer Barnett

While I was processed in the jail, I received all the looks that an actor or singer would have received. Some police even asked if I need anything. I used the phone for over an hour, making many calls when only one is allowed, but they never said get off the phone.

My bond to get out was set at $100,000. The arresting officers were not pleased at this: they knew that I would be out within minutes of this bond being given—plus, my step-father was also a bondsman.

I was out before they finished the paper work and eating at the Waffle House on Sugar Creek. I was also receiving a lot of calls from my female friends, but I just wasn't in the mood to be with anyone. I was trying to figure out what I would do next—I drove home.

This is when "The Two Spencer's" begin to engage each other.

You see, there was "Spencer," the business man: smart, educated, a gentleman, God-fearing, loveable and approachable.

Then there was "Spencer Barnett," (Doc), hustler, bad attitude, mad at all women because of Feet and Cookie, a cheater like my father, and the one, who as long as he had money, didn't need to pray.

The fights between "The Two Spencer's" would go on inside my head. They would fight over every decision that I had to make. "Spencer" wanted to get back into the church, get my family back together, give to the community, and go serve my time in prison.

But the "Spencer Barnett" side would always want to go to Florida, buy the biggest load ever and make money, have women, and say, "Forget praying. I take care of me."

Everyone I loved had their hands out, never asking what I was going through. My brother was becoming a criminal due to his own drug habit, my grandmother was having more headaches then ever and even went through a period of heavy drinking before going cold turkey, and my mother was battling her own demons.

So who would I turn to?

I realized it's true that money doesn't buy happiness. I was not even close to being happy. In fact, I hated my life.

I started blowing money, giving it away.

"Spencer," the good guy, would host basketball tournaments in honor of my cousin Charles Jackson just to use up money and keep him alive.

"Spencer Barnett," the hustler, would pay the lawyer large amounts of money to put off or delay my trial.

After this battle started to become too much, I retreated to The Ranch where I had not been much in last few months. I didn't come out or take any calls for weeks at a time.

"Spencer" was fighting to change back into the shy kid from middle school and "Spencer Barnett" was fighting for the pedestal he had built for himself and wanted to keep.

I wouldn't eat for many days and when I did, it would be a cup of noodles because it was quick and I didn't have to put much energy into making it.

This is the point where I felt like I had every reason to check out on life. I thought I could take the easy way out of this problem because up until this point in my life I had enough happen to me that it would be justified---in my mind, at least.

The "Spencer" side of my brain tried praying, but the "Spencer Barnett" side had gained much strength because there were so many reminders of the past.

"Spencer" was thinking, "Go do what you have to, and move forward with your life."

"Spencer Barnett" was thinking, "Screw that. Check out. There's no way you're going to prison or stop hustling. Do it, do it now!"

I had always been shocked when I heard of people taking their own lives. I didn't understand what could be so bad to make them ever want to do such a sin.

But here I was, thinking what I never even imagined I could think. I remember looking in the medicine cabinet at all the pills that Bippy and I had gotten over the years for different things: toothaches, headaches, many others from her doctor visits, even some from the baby.

I was thinking, "Well, I could just take all these pills because, surely, shooting myself is totally not within my power."

I got all the bottles down and emptied them on the bed and just looked at them.

"Do it, do it now!" I kept hearing from the right side of my head.

"You have a child and family members that love you," the left side of my brain was yelling.

Back and forth. Back and forth. This went on inside my head, to the point of giving me a headache.

I got up and walked out on the deck and started thinking about what my grandmother would always tell me.

"God won't give you more then you can handle," she always said.

I looked up to God.

"Oh, yeah...?" I said. "God, why do you think I'm so strong?

At that very second I turned around and went inside the house. I gathered the pills off the bed and flushed then down the drain.

You see, I realized that it was not God who had given me all this stuff and it wasn't God letting me even think that way. It was the Devil who had given me these things and turned me into who I had become and now he was trying to finish me off.

"No way, no how, you going to win," I said to the Devil.

I knew I had turned my back on God, disregarded everything that I had ever stood for, and did things that I promised to never do.

I had become all of the things I never wanted to be, lost a lot of friends and respect along the way. I use to sit in clubs wondering what people was thinking of me, or how many didn't understand me.

Did they know my childhood? Did they realize I grew up poor or that Feet and Cookie had changed me forever?-- Did they know my father was a cheater with an attitude?

So many questions and so little answers.

Pray Through The Pain

The Lord the Avenger of His People

Plead my cause, O Lord, with those
who strive with me;
Fight against those who fight

against me!

Take hold of the shield and buckler
and stand up for my help!

Also draw out the spear and stop those
who pursue me. Say to my soul," I am your
salvation!"
Let those be put to shame
And brought to dishonor those
who seek after my life!
Let those be turned back
And brought to confusion those who plot my hurt!

Let them be like chaff before the wind
And let the angel of the Lord chase them
Let their way be dark and slippery,
And let the angel of the Lord pursue them.

For without cause they have hidden their net for me in a pit,
Which they have dug without cause for my life
Let destruction come upon him unexpectedly,
And let his net that he has hidden catch himself;
Into that very destruction let him fall

Psalm 35: 1-8

Chapter 24

Walking the green mile

I had been going back and forth to court. There was delay after delay and a lot of paying money to my lawyer, Bill Parks, who had a office down in the Cameron Brown Building on McDowell Street.

Parks was a very sharp guy, really aggressive, and well-respected in the city of Charlotte. He was doing ok on my case, but I felt he could be doing more. I had to constantly stay on him about my well-being. I ended up receiving 10 years which meant I would have to do three years and eight months before parole.

Parks got me some time to turn myself in and get my affairs in order. I spent that time enjoying myself and family, got my bills paid up, and trying to make sure when I was released that I would be fine.

I had to turn myself in to the city of Charlotte to pay my debt for my past criminal activities on

November 20, 1993. I was prepared for this day and wanted to go and get it all behind me.

The morning of my surrender I woke up, prayed, and had a good breakfast before calling my little sister, Shakeena, and my little brother Marvin.

My mother was not living in Charlotte at this time, but had moved to Waynesville to be close to her good friend, Vickie Winston, who she had been friends with as far back as I could remember. She had two daughters and one son there, so she was not in Charlotte on this day.

I picked Shakeena and Marvin up and we headed downtown to the court house where I waited for Bill Parks outside the court room. After some time, he walked up.

"Do you have some money for me?" was the first thing he asked.

"I have paid you all I'm going to pay you," I said, "now let's get this over with."

He went up to the front of the court room and talked with the DA and the Judge. Then I went up and went through the steps of the surrender process.

I looked back at my little sister and winked.

The officers led me to the back of the court room through a door where other inmates were waiting to be hauled over to the jail across the street.

After 23 days downtown, I was to be sent to Piedmont Correctional Facility where I would be processed into the prison system.

The morning of being shipped out, I woke up, looked up at the ceiling, thought to myself, "This is just the first day." I think it finally hit me that I would be under the control of other human beings telling me when to wake, when to shower, and when to eat. This would be a challenge for me considering I had done as I pleased for the last 5 years.

I also knew that my money would have little impact, if any at all, because outside of Charlotte the other prison's didn't know or wouldn't care who I had been on the streets.

I mean news about me was floating around in the city, but I knew that would be pretty much where it would stop. This was fine with me because I just wanted to do my time and move forward with my life.

They rounded up the inmates that were to be shipped out that morning. We were told to pack up our things and were escorted to a big white bus with the words Department of Corrections written on the side in bold black letters.

I boarded this bus knowing I would be leaving Charlotte for some time. I went to the middle of the bus and took a seat near the window and just looked at the heavy armed officers that were guarding the bus.

I noticed one of the officers was one of my old school mates from Garinger High School. He looked at me and smiled as if to say, “You still OK with me.”

I nodded back and the bus began to pull out of the underground garage onto McDowell Street, turning left and then right onto Independence Blvd. We were indeed on our way.

Most of the inmates were talking to each other or sleeping sitting up with their heads bobbing back and forth, awaking as the bus hit bad spots along the road way.

I just sat thinking, “How did I get here from my plan to join the Marines?”

You see, I had come to realize that up until this point in my life I had always done things that others had asked or suggested I do---from the pennies, to going over to Independence High School that day and eventually getting into the drug business. It had all been other people’s ideas.

I had not been a leader, but a follower, and every punishment that I had received, I deserved because I was not thinking for myself in any of those situations.

We arrived at the facility by 11:00AM and were guided through this huge double chain-link fence with barbed wire across the top of it, circling the entire grounds of the prison. We walked in, receiving the stares of the hundreds of inmates already living in the facility, as well as the staff of guards, pastors and nurses.

We went through the processing, showering, the rules, before having shots and being given tests. It was just as I always had seen in the movies and all too much of a reminder of how far off track my life had become.

Chapter 25

The Test

Once you arrive at a prison camp you are given tests for head lice, various diseases, and the big one---an AIDS test.

I had never thought much about disease all through the years because I had the mindset that this only happens to other people, not in my neighborhood, to my friends, or to me. Period.

As I was giving this blood I begin to really think about how many women I had slept with and began to wonder if all of them were clean.

I had had many sleeping partners. I couldn't even begin to think of the random ones I would sleep with from time to time. Also the one night stands—I had a few of them over the years---I couldn't remember their names if my life required telling them now. I would wear condoms, but on many sex-filled nights there were none in sight.

I finished this test and would not know the answer until the blood was sent off to a lab and then a letter sent back with the information---about two weeks later.

Trying to get adjusted to my new life and having to wait on an answer to the AIDS question—that, in all honesty, I didn't know for sure, 100%, what the answer would be---was a mind-wrecking affair.

I had never worried about anything until this came popping into my life and, frankly, it was driving me crazy. I would be up at night retracing my steps. Who looked like there could be something wrong with them? Who were the ones that acted strange after the sex? I could not figure out anything, because what does someone with a disease look like?

I mean every girl I had sex with looked like a normal girl. I couldn't imagine any of them having anything. I tried to relax myself by saying, "There's nothing wrong with me. I look just fine. I'm very healthy for a 23 year old man."

But it always went back to not being sure. Two weeks came and went and I had been waiting on this letter. But, nothing. Every day it was the same---no letter from the lab.

I went up to a prison guard.

"Why have I not received a letter from this bad news lab?"

The guarded looked at me, puzzled.

“When did you have the test?” he said.

“When I was processed in the facility, about three weeks ago,” I said.

“You only get a letter if there is something wrong,” he said, “and the nurse would have sent for you by now to go over information with you about what it was you might have had.”

I raised my eyes.

“Are you sure?” I said.

“Yes,” he said, “you can relax.”

Then he turned and walked away.

I was so relieved to hear that news. I kept playing his words over in my head to make sure I had heard him correctly.

Right then I said to myself, “I will never put myself at risk ever again. I don’t want to have to live through this kind of self worry again.”

I should have known better from the beginning and I would commit to getting checked more often upon my release. I was special and I knew that God gives you one body. I knew I needed to take care of myself from that moment on.

Your body is a temple and you control what and who goes inside you so we need to be educated and safe.

Get Tested!

Chapter 26

The old man on the lower bunk

I spent 28 days at the Piedmont facility. Then I was shipped right back to Charlotte to Camp Green right off the Billy Graham Parkway and Tyvola Road. It looked like some old buildings with a small chain link fence surrounding it. There was a long row of about 20 pay phones and a small workout area near the canteen where goods could purchased and food other than the food in the chow hall.

Outside the fence was the Warden's office and to the right of it was a sitting area full of picnic tables used for inmate visits with friends, lawyers and family members.

This was a minimum security prison for inmates who had less than two years to go on their sentences—there was very little reason for them to try to escape.

I wondered why I had been shipped here so early, but I was very happy to be right back in Charlotte—it meant my family wouldn't have to drive three hours to see me on Sunday anymore.

This prison was very different from Piedmont Correctional and the mood was very different. It was very easy and laid back.

The fence around the prison was only six feet tall, no barbwire or any kind of alarm. Most of the officers were regular guys who just wanted to get through the day without having to deal with a fight or grown men whining about something.

After being processed in, I was given instructions as to where I would be sleeping and working, which would be in the kitchen. I had previous work experience in the restaurant business, so this would be my place of work. I would be earning $7.00 a week, total, for a 35 hour work week.

Working in the kitchen was considered the top job there--it sure beat picking up cigarette butts by hand on the camp ground every morning for three hours.

I was housed in a building with the older guys, which was good considering I was a lot more mature than my age. Most of the guys in the other dorms were 18-25 and they still hadn't gotten everything from the streets out of their systems. It wasn't unusual to see a fight or two daily.

I was bunk mates with this older guy named Rucker from Concord. He had a 12 year sentence for drug trafficking. He was 53 and a nice looking guy for his age---and he had a thing for the ladies. But, he was laid back and very wise.

I started talking to him about my situation and how I was in the streets, but he stopped me and informed me he knew who I was. He let me know that my name had floated around down in Concord. I was surprised by this information, but I just brushed it off and continued listening to him.

"If you want to let everyone know who you are," he said, "and continue in that role, then fine, but it comes with a lot of the same things that controlled you in the streets. Or you can take advantage of the programs here and get your life together. When you're released, you won't have to go hustle anymore and make coming to prison a regular part of your life."

He told me most of the guys there were on their third or fourth sentences or they had been locked up 15-20 years already.

I knew what he was saying was right and I didn't want this for my life. Sleeping in a dorm with 29 other men, showering while others were on the toilet right beside the showers, having to lock everything up---I realized that prison only made you that much more guarded and less trustful of others. I mean some of those guys would steal a cigarette out of your mouth and then ask you for a light.

I made my mind up quickly about how I would use this time: I took every class available to me, kept a low profile and just did my job until I was allowed to go out into the work place on the work release program. Work release allowed you to work in the community during the days and return at night.

I also joined the Think Smart Program. Inmates would go to the local schools and talk to the troubled youths. I always liked doing that and I remembered what my grandmother always told me about giving back.

I liked to talk anyway so it was a great chance for me to try and save someone from the streets or from themselves. I felt like, I owe a lot because I had taken so much—I was the bad guy.

Chapter 27

The promise

One night, riding back to the camp with my boss from Prime Sirloin on Billy Graham Parkway—I had taken a pre-employment training class at the prison, a requirement in order for an inmate to be allowed to go back into the work environment---I was thinking of the direction I had taken with my life.

When I stepped out of his red Toyota Forerunner, I knew that there would be a need for many changes once I was to be released.

“Thank you for the ride,” I said.

I walked up to the gate and rang the bell, letting the guard know someone was outside the gate. It was 1:12AM. It took the guard, who had fallen asleep inside the gatehouse, a few minutes to come and let me inside.

After being patted down, removing my shoes and being asked if I had anything good to eat from the restaurant—not allowed, but they always asked anyway---I went up the walkway.

Once inside my dorm I wasn't sleepy, so I retrieved a cup of noodle soup from my locker, ran hot water into it and went into the day room to watch television.

Everyone had gone to bed, so I had the place all to myself. Flipping the channels and not seeing much of interest to watch, I turned the television off and just played with the soup which had swelled up from me leaving the lid closed too long.

One of my buddies Derrick, had awakened , and was walking to the rest room. He glanced at me and continue to the rest room. He finished his business and approached me in the day room.

"What the H.... you doing in here alone," He asked.

" Nothing man," I said.

"You want me to bust your A... in checkers?" He asked

"Not right now man," I said.

He turned and went back to bed.

I sat at the table looking back into the area that housed the beds, looking at the other 28 inmates sleeping---one guy's bed was empty because he had gotten this great idea to go over to his girlfriend's house instead of work and had gotten himself 30 minutes of pleasure for a trade off of 30 days in the hold.

I was thinking, "This is not the life for me."

I turned to have a conversation with the Big Guy upstairs.

"God," I said, "if You're not so busy, I would like to talk with You for a minute. You see, Lord, I don't belong here. I mean, I owe time for my crime, but I don't want this for my life. I ask that You give me the strength to leave this place and to live the way You have planned for me.

"I make this promise to You, my God, and to myself: I will never sell drugs again or deal in anything that is not of Your blessing. I will lift Your name up everywhere I go, And I ask You, O Lord, to not let me leave this place until You know I am ready.

In JESUS name, AMEN.

Chapter 28

The release

I had my mind set on the three years and eight months that was required on my 10 year sentence, but many of the guys were going home early because of overcrowding.

If you didn't have a violent crime, they were letting some guys out early or giving them longer parole to ease the over-loading of inmates that were coming through the prison system.

I received a letter on October 17, 2005, informing me that I was up for parole. I was confused. I had only been in the system close to two years. I was thinking, "This must be a mistake," but, sure enough, it was indeed true.

I went back into the dorm and showed the letter to Mr. Rucker.

"That's great news," he said. "You should recieve an official letter within a month.

“Really…?” I said.

“Yes, Youngblood,” he said---Youngblood was the name he called me. “Are you ready to live outside of these gates?”

I hadn’t looked at it from that point of view.

For the next few weeks I stayed prayed up and asked God to give me strength to go back out into the world with everything I needed to make it and not come back to this kind of life.

Just as Rucker said, I did receive an early release letter.

Boy, was I surprised. I read the letter over and over making sure I didn’t misread something. But it read the same every time. Finally, I was able to relax, knowing that it was really about to happen.

November 21, 1995, I was called out to the White House, where the Warden’s office was located, outside of the gate. I was pointed to an office and given my release information by the head officer.

After giving all of my information---where would I live? What schools would I attend? What did I plan for work? I was even asked if I would keep the job I had or would I look for a new one.

It was finally here! I would be going home the next day to move forward with my life. I went back on the yard and started getting my things ready for the next day and saying my "good byes" to the few guys that I had become really good friends with. I gave them the things I had no plans to take home with me.

I couldn't sleep that night thinking about what all I needed to do, how I would make money and where I would live. I had a talk with God and I knew that I would be just fine. After finally falling asleep, the morning came and I was all smiles hoping that the parole officer would be on time---they were known for waiting all day to come get you out, just to show you who was in control.

At 2:13PM, I was sitting on the basketball court bench and I saw the white car the parole office always drove pull into the lot.

A short black man exited the vehicle, walked up to the front gate and showed some ID to the guards at the Gate House. The guards, in turn, called my name over the loud speaker telling me to report to the front gate.

I walked down the walkway giving "fist bumps" to the guys who had lined up to see me on my way out of the gate.

I walked out, turning to look back at the two officers who had informed me that they had made a bet---one was betting that I would be back and the other was betting that I wouldn't.

I just shook my head and entered the parole officer's car. He turned to me.

"Do what you are supposed to do," he said, "and I won't have any reason to bring you back to prison."

I just turned away and looked out of the window. Little did he know---I had already promised my God that I would not be back.

It was out of the parole officer's control. His words had no effect on me.

Chapter 29

The pressures of life

I went to live with my grandmother the first two weeks after being released because they wouldn't parole you to yourself. Afterwards, I was allowed to move to my own place in the Coffey Creek Apartments on South Tryon Street.

I was living on the 3rd floor and had to come out to wave to my parole officer because I was on house arrest the first 6 months. I had to be home every night by 8PM and he never wanted to climb the stairs.

I still had a little money saved, but most of it had been stolen, taken by the police or borrowed and not repaid.

Things were very tight and I wasn't making much money working at Prime Sirloin---I mean barely paying the bills. I was using most of the money I saved to make up the difference.

I knew that I would have to downsize soon or I would be going broke. I applied for many good paying jobs, trying to get into a better situation for myself, but, time after time, I would be told, because of my record I couldn't be hired—or, "Were not hiring at this time," which meant the same thing as, "We are not hiring you."

I sold my BMW and bought an old used Subaru for $800. I moved out of the $790 a month two-bedroom apartment to a studio underneath a house owned by Mrs. Jones for $400 a month---all utilities included.

I took some of the money I had and started a cleaning business, part-time, when not at the restaurant. I started taking different little clinics at Home Depot, reading books and watching This Old House on television to learn about the building process. I slowly started building clients.

After about 6 months of building my business, I felt relaxed enough to do it full time. I advised my boss at Prime Sirloin that I would be moving on.

He tried his best to convince me to stay because I had become the assistant manager by then---even offering me more money. But I knew if I were to ever make any real money, I would have to step out on faith.

Although I would be taking a big chance, not having any insurance, plus I had to make sure that

I could provide for my daughter, Mercedes. By now, I had divorced Bippy and was paying child support through the court system I had set up while I was on the work release program.

But I prayed about it and I believed in myself. I knew all the motivation I needed was being broke. I never wanted to be broke.

I knew myself. I knew I would work my butt off trying to stay afloat. I just told myself, “If I hustle running this business like I hustled the streets, I will be just fine.”

The first few years would test me like nothing else. So many times I wanted to throw in the towel and go find another job. It seemed every step forward would be followed by two steps backward.

Many people didn’t want to take a chance on the new guy, a small business owner, but I kept praying and kept doing the best job possible. In the 3rd year things started to really take off and I was not looking back.

Chapter 30

The Goodwill suit

I hadn't found a church home since being released. I was just visiting random churches, but not finding one that felt right for me.

A friend made me aware of this little church down off of North Tyron Street behind the old vinegar factory, near the railroad crossing. It went under the name "Jesus Christ Abundant Life". The church was under the leadership of Pastor Andrew Lockhart and his wife Benita, who both preached very well.

I visited this church and had a very good feeling about the message. I was sold on the idea of this being my church home. I went out the next day to look for some new suits.

I went to the Men's Warehouse where they convinced me to buy three new suits for $299 each as they saw I was going to purchase more than one suit. I had my new suits, a new Bible and a new attitude—well, so I thought!

One Sunday, I woke up in a very good mood: all was well with my life now. My business was doing OK, I was a free man, and the church was a place that I could call my home.

The members were very nice and the preaching was totally new and refreshing. So this particular morning I was in a good space.

I showered in about ten minutes because the water would get cold fairly quick when the tenant on other side showered. I finished dressing, grab a bowl of Corn Pops cereal, and I headed out the door to go to church.

I was driving down Sugar Creek preparing to turn on North Tyron Street, when I noticed a guy with a sign saying, "I will work for food."

I pulled over to the side of the road and got out of my car and walked over to where he was standing with what looked like everything he owned in the world in a shopping cart.

"Hi," I said. "May I ask you a question?"

"Yes, sir," he said, "you may. Do you have work for me?

"No," I said, "but I will give you money."

"I work for my keep," he said, "I don't need a handout."

“Sir,” I said, “I don’t want to give you a handout, I simply want to give you ten dollars. All I ask of you in return is to come join me at my church for the day.”

His eyes were very large by then. He started to shake his head before saying, “I don’t want to go to your church so those fancy dressed people can look down their nose at me.”

“They won’t do that,” I said, “they are very nice people.”

After about ten more minutes of back and forth, I had to go or I would have been late for church myself. I gave him a ten dollar bill.

“You owe me one Sunday,” I said. “I will come looking for you in one week for church.

He nodded his head and said, “Thank you.”

I reached the church, hurried inside and took a seat on the fourth row beside one of the assistant pastors who turned to talk to me. The conversation with the homeless guy was fresh on my mind and I shared it all with the pastor.

“Maybe I can understand where he is coming from,” I said.

He looked at me with a very straight face.

“When was the last time you had to worry about your clothes?” he said.

I was in shock at that moment and said nothing.

"You have on a nice suit," he continued. "May I ask how much you paid for it?"

"$299," I said with a little pride. "I have three new ones."

"Why did you feel that you had to have a $299 suit?" he said. "Are you here for The Word or here to show that you are still rich and caught up in the world of material things which was your downfall before?"

There was nothing that I could say because what he said hit a nerve. I had never looked at it from that point of view. I sat quietly the rest of the service, a little confused.

Afterwards some of the younger members were going over to Church's Chicken for dinner and asked me to join them, but I wasn't in the mood. I headed home to watch a little bit of television, but there wasn't anything on and I couldn't get the events of the day out of my head.

I prayed and went to bed, but I tossed and turned for the first two hours and then, finally, I fell asleep.

The next morning I knew what I had to do. I put on my sweatpants and shoes and headed straight out of the door---no breakfast, shower or brushed teeth. I drove to the Goodwill on Albemarle Road across from the Wal-Mart.

I went inside with the three suits I had purchased for church and donated them. Then I purchased a suit for twelve dollars and two pairs of pants for twenty-five dollars.

I knew that this suit would humble me and keep me focused on what I needed to do. You see, I had learned a few things the day before:

1. Most people don't come to church because they feel the members will look down upon them.

2. Don't say you understand where someone is coming from if you haven't been there.

3. I don't need to have a $299 suit to go church---what I need is to go and listen, fellowship, and get The Word.

Stage 4:

Now I know in part;
then I shall know fully,
even as I have been fully known.

Chapter 31

The Latino girl

Driving on South Tyron Street about to reach the light at Woodlawn, I said to myself, "If I reach the light before it turns red, I will go straight through and get on Highway 77. If it turns red then I will turn right on red and go down Woodlawn Avenue."

I made it to the light and it had just turned yellow, so I continued straight and bore right onto the Highway 77 bypass. As I was about to pass the Animal Shelter and the Clinton Road exit, I noticed a burgundy Toyota Corolla with a very pretty Latino girl driving alone. She seemed to be in a hurry because she was far exceeding the speed limit.

I looked over at her and to my surprise she smiled at me. I smiled back and didn't think much of it. But, as I continued down the freeway, I noticed we kept ending up right beside each other. Once again, we smiled at each other.

She then began to drive even faster, so I made it a point to keep up with her---I guess you could say it was a little “cat and mouse chase.”

We rounded the exit going onto where they would later build Panthers Stadium. I was in the left lane and she was two lanes over on the right.

I held my phone up indicating that I wanted her phone number. She then held up her phone to signal back that she had one. I pulled into the same lane behind her and followed her off the ramp near CPCC--Central Piedmont Community College. She continued on and didn’t stop. I continued to follow until the light caught me.

I remember thinking to myself, “I guess I’m not getting her number today.”

But then I saw her brake light come on. She was moving slow, but not getting out of my sight. Once my light turned green, I caught up to her as she was making a right into the CPCC parking lot.

I followed her inside the lot. I pulled behind her car and she exited and walked over to my car.

“Hi,” we both said---and that’s pretty much all we understood besides giving away our cell phone numbers.

She was attending CPCC to learn English and it was clear that she had just begun the class. She was a very pretty lady, with a big smile and looked as if she could be a decoy for Jennifer Lopez.

I didn't call her, thinking that if she was serious then she would give me a call---but the call never came. A few days passed and still no call from her.

I thought, "Well, let me at least see if this is the real number."

I dialed the number and she answered the call.

"It's Spencer," I said, "the guy that met you at the college."

"Yes," she said. "How are you?"

"I have been fine," I said. I must say, I was a little surprised to know it was indeed the right number.

We talked for some time and I don't think we really understood each other, but somehow we planned a movie date for the following Tuesday.

I met her in the CPCC parking lot where she left her car and we headed out to see a movie at the Delta 6 on W. T. Harris Blvd.

It was a Tuesday night so there wasn't anyone inside the movie---we had the theater all to ourselves. After the movie finished I stood up to walk out and turned to hug her. When I hugged her, I had to bend down because she was very short---maybe 5 feet---and our faces touched.

I was pulling away and she turned her head, lining her lips with mine and began kissing me. Then, after a very passionate kiss, we pulled back and just smiled at each other and turned to exit theater without saying anything.

It was very cold that night, so as we walked back to my Land rover, she was shaking. I put my arm around her and walked her to the passenger side of the car and opened her door.

I came back around to the driver's side and entered the car. I started the car to allow it to warm up and I noticed she was still shaking. So I reached over and hugged her again.

After about five minutes the car was nice and warm, but she kept holding me, so I just relaxed and continued to hold her, not saying much, because we still didn't understand each other very well. It was just a very silent moment and it was very nice.

I drove her back to her car and we headed out in different directions. We dated a few more times, the talking getting better each time we saw one another. Then, one day, she just completely disappeared--no calls, not answering her phone, not even being in the school parking lot. For about a week—nothing.

I was thinking, "What happened to her? Maybe she didn't like me or maybe she's married or something."

Then one night I called her again, saying to myself, “This will be the last time I’m going to try.”

She picked up the phone, but didn’t say anything.

“Hello... hello,” I kept saying. “If you want me to stop calling, just let me know something.”

Still she said nothing.

“I will let you go now,” I said, “since you are not talking back to me. Goodbye.”

She hung up the phone and I sat on the chair thinking to myself, “This lady is strange.”

But, the only thing was, I really liked her.

Two nights later, I was sleeping in my chair downstairs. Around 2:00AM my cell phone began to ring, I looked at it and the name on the ID said Gloria, so I answered it.

But once again, she didn’t say anything, just listened to me asking a million questions. Then she just said goodbye.

I was home after work three days later, just relaxing, watching television and there was a knock on my door. I was surprised, because I wasn’t expecting anyone that day.

I went to the door and pulled it open. There Gloria stood.

I couldn't say anything. For one reason, I couldn't believe it was her, and, two, I was surprised she remembered how to come to my house considering she had been there only once and I lived far out—not easy to remember.

But there she stood. I opened the storm door and she walked inside and stood in the dining room.

"Hi," I said. "How are you?"

"Hi," she said back.

"You OK?" I said. "Everything alright?"

"Yes," Gloria said. "I was not understand you, Papi." She had started calling me Papi which is Spanish for Daddy.

"I see," I said. "I was thinking you didn't like me."

"No," she said, "I like you very much so."

She was still learning to put her words together.

"OK, cool," I said. "Are you hungry? I will make you some food."

"Si, Papi," she said.

I made us some chicken breast, mashed potatoes and green beans. We sat down and had dinner.

We dated for one year and began living together. It all seemed so perfect. For the first time in my life, I really felt like this could be the one---the one who could keep my attention and love me with all she had.

You see, up until this point, and because of lingering feelings about my past, I had never been with anyone I felt like I could be faithful to. I knew that I wasn't going to let this one get away.

One Saturday when Gloria was at her job, I went to Browne Lee Jewelry Store on Park Road and I picked out what I thought would be a great engagement ring.

Later that evening we went to dinner and I asked her if she wanted to go for a walk by the lake, in the university area.

"I would like that a lot, Papi," she said.

I drove over to the lake and we went walking, holding hands. It was a very beautiful night, nice and calm. We walked for about ten minutes. When we were half way around the lake, I stopped.

"Hold on," I said. "Let me tie my shoe."

She stopped in front of me, looking at the moon light glowing off of the lake surface. But then she turned, wondering why I was taking so long to tie my shoe.

I was down one knee with the ring out, looking up at her. I took a hold of her hand. She was totally in shock and began covering her mouth.

"Oh, my God, Papi…oh, my God," she kept saying, "Oh, my God."

"You have changed my life," I said, "and I have never met anyone like you. You make my life worth living. I believe, without any doubt, that I have met my soul mate. I love you with all that I am, and I want to spend the rest of my life with you. I want to know: will you marry me?

"Si, Papi," she said. "Yes...yes...yes.

Chapter 32

Temptations

You ever notice that as soon as you get married everything is great, but that's when women seem to notice you more---or at least you think so?

Or when your money starts to look a little short for the next thing you want, then you start thinking, "Now how quick can I get some money?"

Becoming stronger with God has kept me away from a lot of this type of temptation. I'm still human and have and will make mistakes, but I'm a lot wiser now then I was twenty years ago. I think of more than just myself and my personal happiness when making decisions.

There were times when my wife and I would be dinning out at Restaurants, I would catch women stealing quick glances my way. Not just once but several times. I don't know if I'm making too much of these glances, but the player part of my life is in the past. I love my wife too much to disrespect her in public or anywhere else.

When people confide in me, asking me for guidance, I talk and listen to them as a friend. One woman misunderstood my friendly nature and took it the wrong way. She called me in the middle of the night asking me to come over. I was quick to respond to her that I was simply being a friend and giving her guidance in her time of need—and that there were no hints of anything further than friendship. I specified to her if I was to continue being a friend to her, it would strictly be on a professional basis, no more phone calls to my private cell.

From that day on, I have learnt not to give my private number out to anyone, if they wish to confide in me, email or write to me and I will respond professionally, and efficiently.

In life, you learn through your own mistakes--my mistake at that time was, I trusted people to much with my friendship, and in the process the boundaries were overstepped. We are still friends, but we are in a new space now and sometimes it's hard to give them advice considering how we got there.

One day, a good buddy of mine who has a car dealership called to inform me he had a Mercedes---

my car of choice--with my name written on it. I went to give it a test drive.

Driving down Independence Blvd. in the black-on- black s500---my favorite---with chrome wheels, the car felt good in my hands. It had a nice tight ride and had low mileage. I had one at home, but it was older.

I'm thinking, "It's time to upgrade. The other one has a few miles on it, plus it's been in a wreck."

You get a lot of looks in an expensive car--not just from woman--but just in general. I never get these looks in my Dodge Ram pickup.

Sometimes we try to become one with our cars, and we begin to think that's how we are measured.

But the real question is---what or who are we without the car beside us?

I used to buy cars as a sign of status and because they made me feel better about myself---or, at least, I thought so. I buy a car now simply because I like it and get a good deal on it.

I have seen many of my friends cars get them in a lot of trouble because the attention that came with their cars.

Terry, my buddy, is the owner of Custom Auto works on Central Avenue. I took the Mercedes over to let Terry take a look. I saw another friend(willie) there in his new car. We were standing around talking about motorcycles and old times. By his conversation, I could easily tell he was still hustling.

"Let me holla' at you for a minute, Doc," he said. He still called me by my old name.

We walked outside and were standing beside his drop-top BMW with everything you could name in it or on it--all the latest equipment.

"I got these people who can give you a good deal on some work," he said.

I just looked at him, because I knew what he meant. He continued on about it was a great deal and would be quick money.

"No, man, that's not my thing anymore," I said.

"I'm a business man now and my company is doing very well."

"I respect that, man." he said.

"Nice seeing you, man," I said. "I'm heading over to the dealership to take this car back."

Sometimes we are faced with very challenging temptations in our life. Sometimes this requires people--old friends, especially--getting answers they do not want or understand.

That's how life is sometimes.

Chapter 33

Why God?

Every time my life started to go well, there was always something bad to follow. It was just the way things always seemed to happen in my life.

Here I was now, happily married with two beautiful daughters at home. My business was at an all time high and I was at peace with my life at this point.

One day, I was at home cutting my grass---it had grown long because I had been very busy for three weeks and had not gotten around to getting it done. My wife came to the door with the cordless phone in her hand and motioned to me.

"Why?" I asked as I walked toward her. "Who is it?"

"It's your mother," she said.

I reached the door as she pushed it open, grabbed the phone, looked down, and wiped my feet as I entered the house and greeted my mother.

"What's going on?" I said.

"It's Mama," she said. "Can you come over to her house?"

"Yes, but---" I said. "I'm on the way."

"What's wrong?" my wife asked me.

"I don't know! I'll be right back."

"You want me to go with you?" she asked.

"No…No. I'll be back soon."

I got in my car and headed over to my grandmother's house. She had moved to the Plaza area on Harwyn Avenue because the city had torn down Earle Village, her old apartments, and was in the process of building new mixed-use apartments and shops, trying to attach more middle-class people to the downtown area.

Charlotte was going through a very aggressive growth period due to two of the biggest banks having headquarters based in Charlotte. A huge amount of money was being spent.

When I was driving down Milton Road, all kinds of things went through my head. I was talking to God saying, "Things are ok, right? Please, let everything be ok."

I turned my car onto my grandmother's street and looked far ahead, trying to see if there were many cars down the hill in front of my grandmother's house.

Pretty much everyone's car that I could think of was in the driveway, on the grass, and on the street. I pulled up, exited the car and walked passed my cousin, Wanda, standing in the front yard smoking on a Newport cigarette.

"Hi, big cuz," she said.

"Hi, Wanda," I said. "What's up?"

Shaking her head, she pointed to the door. I went inside and most of the family was there.

"What's wrong?" I said. "Where is Mama?"

"She in the hospital right now," my aunt Linda said

"What's wrong with her?" I said.

"She suffered a stroke," she said, "and not doing well."

"But she going to be OK, right?"

"We don't know."

"Can we go see her?" I said. "Who is over there with her now?"

"Patricia, your mom and Oscar are over there right now," Aunt Linda said, "they going to call back with more information soon."

We all just sat around trying to be positive---even though, I know, we all were thinking the worst in our heads.

Oscar called saying that Mama was doing a little better, but they had done all they could do for her. So for the next two weeks we all were back and forth over to the hospital.

It was May 29th 1997, when they told us that she would be allowed to come home. We were all happy because her 63rd birthday was coming up on June 6th. We wanted her to be home for her birthday.

I was over at the Chicken Coop getting some of the famous chicken and my favorite iced tea, making sure to tell the lady to hold the ice because she would fill the cups with crushed ice and then I wouldn't get much tea.

I was going to get my food and head over to pick up Mercedes and take her shopping two days before her birthday which was on June, 5th, a day before my grandmother's.

I received a phone call from my Aunt Peaches saying, "Mama is home."

"Tell her I will be over to see her after I finish shopping for Mercedes birthday gifts," I said.

After going to four different stores and then ending back at the first store again, Mercedes was satisfied with her choices for herself. I drove

Mercedes to her home over off South Blvd, down behind the skating rink. She and her mother were living with Money and her family for a while.

I headed up 77 Highway, then onto I-85. I exited onto Sugar Creek, turned left on The Plaza and right onto Harwyn Avenue. For some reason I had butterflies in my stomach. I wanted to say the right things to my grandmother.

Once inside, my Uncle Kenny sat on the living room coffee table trying to explain to me that he and Tony had been fighting. It was clear that both had too much to drink that day.

“Give me a minute,” I said to him, “I will talk you after I see Mama.”

I continued back to my grandmother’s bedroom where she was sitting on the edge of her bed.

“Hi, old girl!” I said. “You doing OK?

“Hi, baby,” she said. “I’m fine.”

“You gave me a scare.” I said.

“I gave myself a scare.”

I sat down beside her and hugged her tight.

“What you want for your birthday?” I asked her.

“You just gave it to me,” she said. “ you just gave it to me”

We talked for some time and then I informed her that I needed to go because I had to stop by the store before it got too late. I stood to leave.

"OK, baby," she said. "I love you."

I looked back at her and winked---that little thing that we would do. She smiled and I headed to the store.

I was very happy my grandmother was home and I was thinking that she would be fine.

This happiness was short-lived because she passed away 8 days later, after my mother had come home from working the night shift and finding her—she had also been the one who had found her the first time she went to the hospital. I can only imagine how tough it most of been for my mother.

I must admit that I was very upset with God.

I would think, "You took my grandmother away from me? Why? Why now?

I had to do a lot of praying and soul searching.

Then God came to me and said,

I know you think you need her, but I need her more. Now is the time to take what she shared with you during her time on earth and you live.

YOU LIVE!

Chapter 34

God's plan for you

Eating lunch with my little sister, Shakeena, at the Coffee Cup restaurant downtown, I had a lot on my mind. I wasn't talking much.

"What's going on?" she asked me.

Because she knows me better than anyone else and because she and I have a very special bond, this is what I was able to express to her:

"I am dealing with what my place in the world is and what it is I'm supposed to be doing."

I told her I knew my grandmother was in a better place, but I still thought of her daily. I always had a very close relationship with her.

Growing up, I heard talk that my grandmother wasn't pleased my mother was having a baby so young. As a child, I assumed my grandmother didn't want me to be born. I talked to her about it when I was 14.

I was totally relieved when she said it was never about me, just that she was surprised at the time. The most important thing, she said, was the fact she said she wouldn't trade me for the world now.

That's when the winks between us started.

The following Sunday, I was getting ready for church as always and hurrying everyone up, because I live with all women and they are very good at being late.

I was still stuck in the day-before thoughts, and I didn't have the best attitude during this time. After returning back to the house to get the Bible that I left, we were on the way to the church.

The kids were carrying on in the car. My wife was still applying make-up in the mirror on the passenger side. I was deep in my thoughts.

We arrived at the church and hurried inside because the service had begun. We walked down the aisle, to the middle row, where my mother had saved us seats. This was clearly making Sister Williams upset---I could tell by the look on her face as we sat down.

The preacher was talking about personal responsibility and ownership, owning up to our own failures in the community and to family.

He asked us to stand and instructed us to rub our stomach to stir up what God was feeding us. After he finished that section of his sermon, everyone had stopped rubbing their stomachs, but I continued, not even realizing I was still doing it---but I knew I needed a few extra stirs.

The preacher stopped in the middle of his sermon and asked me to come up to the front steps of the church stage. I did, but I was hesitating, clearly curious about why he was calling me up.

He asked me to stand in front of him as the deacons stood behind me. He began to pray over me with his left hand placed upon my forehead. I fell backwards with no force from the preacher.

I must admit that when I would see other people fall back, I always felt like they were faking—but, sure enough, I fell on my own, just flowed back.

After I had been down there a while, feeling God all over me, I sat up and the deacon helped me to my feet.

“Young man,” he said, “I don’t know your story, but I know what God told me.”

He said there was a glow over my life. He let me know God has a special plan for me. He turned me around to face the people in the church.

“This guy is going to be someone important one day,” he said through his cordless microphone. “Take a good look at him.”

Everyone began to clap and praise God. I had no idea what to think of this, so I just said nothing.

“Do you understand what he meant?” I said to my mother when I returned to my seat.

“That’s for you,” she said to me. “God will give you the answer to this question in due time. You have to just wait.”

Chapter 35

The man in the mirror

Three years had passed since the day of the church scene in which I was called to the front---and I was still just as lost as ever.

Not having really figured out my place in the world after such an unusual beginning, it was as if I was caught in the matrix---red or blue pill---and I knew there had to be more to my life than work and home.

I mean, I had a beautiful family and my company was doing well. But there was that something missing and I couldn't figure it out.

One night the family and I were home watching American Idol, this new show about discovering new talent by letting the American public decide by calling in to vote to decide the winners.

I didn't know if America would get it right. I mean, most people would simply vote for their favorite regardless of how they performed week to week.

I began thinking to myself, “What if I didn’t get it right, this thing we called Life and all that it includes?”

The next day I was supposed to build a fence for a lady on Sardis Road. Well, the day didn’t start off very well. First of all, the guys were late, and one was hung over from the night before. Besides this, the transmission in one of the trucks was all but gone causing us to make two trips to the Home Depot on Wendover which meant a late start.

We dug the first six of 32 holes, but then we hit a water pipe and water gushed out--the city had marked the wrong spots on the ground. After the city came and stopped the leak, they informed me I would be receiving a bill from the city of Charlotte.

My phone rang.

“How is your day going?” my wife asked.

“We didn’t get it right,” I said.

As soon as I said that, the same thought I had had the night before while watching American Idol, went through my head, “What if I don’t get it right?”

Later that afternoon, not being able to get anything done because of the burst pipe, we called it a day and I dropped the guys off at Wayne’s Supermarket on Graham Street---and headed home.

I arrived home around 2:30PM and no one was home yet because school wasn't out until 3:15 for Madison and 3:25 for Ashley.

My wife was at her mother's house getting some things together to send back to Honduras for the kids there---and eating because she was pregnant with our third child, Sydney---I had already picked her name---after my favorite actor, Sidney Poitier.

I jumped in and out of the shower, got cleaned up and was brushing my teeth when I looked in the mirror and saw myself for the very first time.

"Who are you?" I said, looking directly at myself.

I was thinking about Sidney Poitier's book The Measure of a Man and the journey he had taken to America, the things he experienced and then he went on to become, in my opinion, the Best Actor Ever.

I was thinking to myself, "Spencer, how do you measure yourself as a man? What is your purpose? What are you supposed to be doing?"

"God," I said, "tell me what it is that I'm supposed to be doing. I mean, all I really know how to do is hustle."

As I stood there applying lotion to my legs—they required a lot, due to dry skin--words started to pop into my head.

"Use what I gave you! Use what I gave you! Use your mouth. People will listen to you. You're not talking fast, they're just listening slow. Let them catch up to you. Give of yourself. Lift My Name up everywhere you go. You can never give too much of yourself when helping people.

It was then I knew what the preacher had told me three years before was becoming clearer.

It was then I knew who the real Spencer was and what I needed to do in this lifetime.

Chapter 36

I am still my father's son

My brother Marvin came over to change the oil in my work trucks. He was a shade-tree mechanic and part-time hustler. He informed me our father had come by his place. I didn't react to what he said and continued talking about the Lakers chances of winning a championship that year.

Four days later I was home helping Ashley with her math homework. She wasn't getting the answers right and it was driving me crazy. I raised my voice in frustration and she looked at me in surprise because I had never done that before.

I got up, went to the restroom, and put water on my face. I returned to the table where she was still sitting. I realized that I needed to be little more patient. I was thinking about my father never being around to help me with my homework.

"I'm sorry, baby," I said.

"That's OK, Daddy," she said.

"Let's get some air, then come back and finish."

"OK," she said. "Let me get my shoes."

Twenty minutes later we were back. When we walked in the house, Madison was standing in the foyer with the telephone in her hand.

"It's for you, Daddy," she said.

"Mr. Barnett?" a strange voice said. "I'm Judy Davis from the Carolina Medical Center. Your father just had an operation on his feet. He indicated to me that you are estranged, but he has nowhere to go.

"He can't come here, Mrs. Davis." I said. "I'm sorry."

"I understand, Mr. Barnett," she said.

One month later, I was going over to my brother's house on Academy Avenue up behind Garinger High School, a little green house on the corner with no grass and oil spots on the driveway.

I arrived there at his house and my brother, Uncle Kenny, and few of their friends were outside working on a Honda Accord. My brother had bought the car for $300 from a guy who was short on his rent payment. They were fixing the carburetor and the radio.

I got out and started talking to the guys. A few minutes later my father exited my brother's back door.

"How are you doing?" I said.

"OK," he said, "But I haven't had a job in some time."

He asked how my business was going, and informed me he would be willing to help me some days if I was short of help.

"I will think about it," I said.

Driving home I began thinking about what my father had done to my mother. I thought about how he was never around for anything that had happened in my life--not once showing up for a game or talent show. He had never seen my wife and kids. He didn't know their names or ages.

I realized that I would never have peace until I addressed the issues that had pushed me away from him. But, I didn't want to focus on it right then.

I thought, "OK, give him a job and get to know him slowly because at this point we were not even in the right space to be father and son."

Soon after, I let him know that he could help me out on the weekends sometimes and he was very thrilled at the idea. He was living at my brother's, so I would simply pick him up there.

In the beginning everything was fine, but soon he had a problem listening to the foreman--he assumed, since he was my dad, he didn't have to listen to this guy. In addition, on jobsites, he always wanted to argue about which way to do things.

I fired and rehired him many times.

I looked at this new situation with my father as if I was doing him a favor. I mean, it's weird how God brings people back together. Here my father was working for the son he never cheered for at a football game, helped with homework. He never even explained the sexual encounter I had witnessed as a child.

I realized soon enough that we could not work together because of his attitude and the fact I still hadn't fully forgiven him. I knew that we would never be father and son like we were when I was a child, but we could start a new relationship. I knew that in order for us to have a chance, we had to take working together out of the equation.

I never asked my father about his infidelities because I figured I made him suffer enough throughout all the years. I did not give him any opportunities. Now, I can clearly see he was trying to reach out to me many times.

I have seen so many of the fathers of my friends pass away without making peace with their sons. I have witnessed my friends' regrets for not mending their relationships with their fathers. I did not want this for myself.

I looked to God to give me the strength to rebuild that father and son relationship.

I had to forgive him. Then, I had to forgive myself.

After all, I am still my father's son.

Chapter 37

Dates with my Daughters

Friday evenings, Mercedes and Briana would come over for the weekend--just imagine six women in one house. One day, I came upstairs and Mercedes was having a pretty loud conversation with someone on her cell phone.

"It's that serious?" I said.

"I'm sorry, Daddy. He's driving me crazy," she said.

I figured this would be as good a time as any to talk to these young ladies. I asked them all to come into the kitchen and to take a seat at the kitchen table.

"You are too young to be getting that upset with that young man," I said, "who's not even your husband yet."

Mercedes just looked at me. I gave her a look back as if to say, "Did you hear me?"

"I hear you, Daddy," she said.

"I used to be the bad guy," I said. "I want to tell you girls about how I used to be and give you everything a guy will use on you or against you to trick you---or to get what he wants out of you. There is not one better person to tell you this then me because I was the best at it and it was wrong.

"You guys are very beautiful and smart," I continued. "You don't need anyone telling you this just to get something---it's not new. I tell you guys this all the time, so don't fall for it. It's nice to hear flattering words, but it should not come with strings attached.

"I'm proud of all of you, but when you guys are out, remember what your last names are. I take this very seriously. You will not be little my name or the Barnett legacy. Have respect for yourselves and make sure others respect you as well."

They were listening.

"I know you guys are at the age where young men are taking interest in you. I can't stop this, but I can teach you how a man should treat you."

Mercedes phone went off.

"Give it to me, please," I said.

I looked at her phone tagline—"Mrs. Miller," it said. She had set it to say that on all the texts she sent out.

“I don’t want to see you using Mrs. Miller.” He’s not your husband I told her, “until you are married. You are only 19 and in your first year of college. You have received a full scholarship because of your grades and you were a track star at West Charlotte High School. You did all of that on your own, no guy helped you achieve that, stay focused. You need to keep your eyes on your long-term goal of becoming a lawyer.”

I didn’t like the idea of some young guy having her so angry she was arguing out loud. I didn’t want her having his name on the end of all her texting. I didn’t want her to lose her focus in school.

That day, I addressed other things with the girls.

“I will start taking you out on one-on-one dates,” I said. “Father and daughter dates. I want to teach you how a young man should treat you. I will test you along the way by saying something inappropriate to see how you react or if you correct me.

I showed them how a young man should open the door for them and how he should push the chair up for them when they sit down at a table.

“A guy gets really good when he can order your food for you,” I told them, “and it’s something you would have picked for yourself.”

I went to eat with Ashley one night at The Olive Garden.

"Daddy," she said, "A guy is saying to me that if I love him I will skip school and hang out with him."

I asked her a few questions about him and from what I gathered he was not going to school and he was only 15.

"You're only 14, Ashley," I told her. "You are not allowed to date now. Try to understand---a young man not going to school is one thing, but a young man trying to get you to miss out on your education is even worse. If he choose to waste his life, or if his parents are not involved in his life---that is very unfortunate.

"These kinds of decision will impact his life later--and his future wife also. I hope that he gets the guidance he needs to get back on track.

"I need you to think about what it is you want for your life."

She seemed to understand the lesson in all of it and quickly informed me that she wanted more for her life.

I am honored that she trusted me enough to confide in me about this guy. We have built a close father and daughter bond. She is comfortable in discussing personal matters with me.

Spend time with your daughters, fathers. Teach them how a young man should treat a young lady. Teach your sons how to treat a woman. We have to break the cycles of the past.

Chapter 38

I Was So Proud

One day in June, 2008, I woke up excited because 39 years after her dream began, my mother was going to graduate with an MBA in Theology from Shaw University in Raleigh, North Carolina.

Since my mother was nine years old, her life had been sad. She had to take care of all her 3 brothers and 5 sisters. There were occasions when my grandparents would be out on the weekends, getting drunk, while my mother would be at home tending to all the kids.

She was not able to attend her prom, try out to be a cheerleader. She wasn't able to hang out with her friends, or just be a normal kid like everyone else. Obviously, she did not get much love and affection from her parents then.

When the first guy came along, telling her she was pretty and paying attention to her, she fell head over heels for him. In the process got pregnant with me and had to drop out of school. Not having many family members to turn to, my mother confided in a counselor that was provided by the school. My mother always had a great respect for education.

And, so, here it was--a great day for my mother's kids and grandkids because she was proving to everyone that she was able to accomplish her goals--even at this late stage in her life.

Once I got everyone organized and ready in the car, I began telling the kids how proud I was of their grandmother, and that no matter what age you are, you can still accomplish your goals---no matter how many years it takes to achieve these goals.

After enduring a long three and a half hour drive---with the kids constantly asking "ARE WE THERE YET?" and Sydney, who was two at the time, in need of a diaper change a few times, due to her stinking the car out with her No. 2's---we finally arrived in Raleigh.

The car park was full and I was thinking to myself there must be a lot of people graduating today as well as my mother. We walked inside the coliseum. I saw many happy and proud people waiting for the graduation ceremony to begin. It was a relaxing atmosphere filled with laughter and joy.

We took our seats and listened as the band played the National Anthem, indicating that the ceremony was about to commence. The guest speaker delivered his congratulations before turning the podium over to the Dean.

The Dean made a brief statement before the graduating students were called to stage. One by one their names were called to receive their diplomas. Some quietly accepted their Diplomas, some step-danced upon receiving theirs, and others were praising God.

I saw my mother reaching the top of the stairs and I knew her name would be called next.

"Annie Marie Davis" the announcer said.

My sister and I---along with all our relatives that came along to witness my mother's graduation---clapped with happiness and erupted with loud cheers.

It was one of the proudest moments of my life.

"That's my Mama" I shouted.

They called a few more names after my mother, before stopping. We all wondered why, when it was clear there were many more people waiting to accept their Diplomas. I looked down towards the stage, and noticed two guys helping a little old lady up the stairs.

"Here is one of my proudest graduates today," the Dean said. "She is 81 years old. She made a promise to her belated husband that she would get her Degree one day."

"Will you be using your degree to get a job?" He asked the old lady.

"No," she said, "but a promise is a promise."

I was totally amazed. Her comment inspired me to see that no matter how old you are, it is a good thing to uphold a promise and see it through. It just blew me away.

This moment gave me the push and motivation I needed to continue pursuing my dreams. I was so happy that my children were there to witness their own grandmother and an 81 year-old lady achieve what they set out to do.

We went to celebrate my mother's graduation at Ryan's Restaurant. I stopped everybody in the middle of their conversations to toast to my mother.

"Mother," I said, "I want to let you know that I'm so proud of you. You endured so much at a young age, even after having me, but you rearranged your life to provide the best that you can for us.

"Through it all, you still managed to follow your dreams to get the degree you rightfully deserve," I said.

Sometimes when we are dealt detours in the road of life---or if there is a road block---we tend to give up. Or we don't look for another route.

Don't ever give up because you can always pave your own road---or simply wait for the road to clear. The road always clears.

Chapter 39

He saved me

April 29, 2009, was a day that changed a lot for me. I was putting the tools on my truck and trying to get the guys to finish picking up the trash so that we could go home early.

I wasn't in the best mood. My wife and I had a heated conversation on the phone about me being on the laptop so much and working so late. I didn't understand why she was upset because I was working--even when I got home I still had to call back clients or be up ordering things for the next day's job. Sometimes I was up pretty late.

After paying the guys, they let me know that they were going to walk to the bus stop because we were working on Laurel Avenue near Presbyterian Hospital. Then I wrote the home owner a receipt and she paid me for the retaining wall we had built in her back yard.

I was driving down Monroe Road, still thinking about the conversation I had had with my wife, still a little upset at the idea of her being mad at me for working late sometimes.

I stopped at Bojangles, got a large cherry soda and two sweet potato pies and headed left down by Cricket Arena onto Independence Blvd. Driving along listening to the radio, I received a text from my sister asking me to cut her grass. I texted her back that I would get to her yard the next day.

I reached Harrisburg Road, made a left at the light and continued down the road. It was a very pretty day out, the sun was shining and there was calm in the air. I passed the new Jehovah Witness church on the right. Looking farther ahead I noticed a white Honda Accord approaching on the opposite side of the road. It seemed to be going at a high speed. Then I saw the car, with a woman driving, start skidding to the right. She tried to correct the car, but she over- corrected and the car begin skidding sideways down the road.

As I watched this car approach---almost sideways at a high rate of speed---I knew she was going the hit me. It seemed like the car was coming in slow motion. So many things went through my mind.

I realized that the last thing I said to my wife was in a fight about me working and being mad at her. I thought about my children who I was going to take to see a movie. I thought about the people that died on 9/11. I thought about all those people who had no idea what was about to happen that day.

I began talking to God.

"Is this how it ends for me?" I said. "Why now, God? You let me reach 40 years old back in March and, now, that's it for me?"

The car was right in front of my Ford Expedition turned sideways. I turned my wheel to the right, hitting a mail box because it was a two-lane road. I raised my left arm to shield my face and braced for the impact.

Again I thought, "Is this how it ends for me?"

As the car hit me everything sped up and the noise was loud. I heard metal scraping, things flying by and a hard blow to my body.

As the other car hit the front of my SUV sideways, it continued its spin after slamming into my car and went back out into the middle of the road.

I realized I was not dead.

I raised my head and observed smoke everywhere and the fumes of gas were in the air. I tried to look left to locate the other vehicle but my head and neck hurt like nothing I had ever felt before. I had no idea where the other car was or if they were OK or not.

I looked up, saying, "Thank you, God, for saving my life. You are giving me more time on earth, more time with my family and more time to get it right."

I thought about my grandmother's death, my last words to her which were so good. I thought about how I would have hated for a silly fight with my wife about working so much and fighting on the phone to have been the last things we said to each other.

The airbags were both out, glass everywhere, and my left arm was badly bruised. My head was pounding and I was dizzy and I seemed like I was sweating on the inside. I wasn't sure if my arm was broken or not, but it really hurt and I couldn't move it. My left leg was bruised and swollen.

I heard the voice of a lady to my left.

"Are you OK?" she asked.

"I'm not sure," I said.

"I'm a nurse," she said. "Where do you hurt?"

"Everywhere."

"OK, don't move," she said. "The medics are on the way."

I heard many vehicles and sirens, then the nurse explaining my injuries to the medics, more of what I had shared with her in more detail as she talked to me to keep me calm and relaxed. Others were with the other driver involved in the accident.

The firemen bent my door open because it had been jammed. They turned me to the left and laid me on the wooden board that they use when trying to be careful of neck or back injuries. Then I was lifted onto the bed and rolled to the ambulance door.

My wife was there because I was just a block from my house. One of the kids from the neighborhood noticed it was my car in the accident and had texted Ashley's cell phone.

Not wanting to believe it was really her dad's car, Ashley asked the kid give her a description. He knew it was my car, he said, because he noticed the chrome 20-inch wheels when it was parked in our driveway. He was 100% sure it was me, he told her.

Now she looked down at me, holding my hand and asked if I was OK. On her face she had a look of so much worry and concern. I wanted her to relax, so I nodded my head and smiled.

I was lifted up into the ambulance and all of my reflexes were checked. They secured me for the ride to the hospital. My wife was in the front of the ambulance and we headed over to Presbyterian Matthews.

Every bump in the road hurt my body and my head was hurting even more. Looking up at the ceiling all I could see was that car coming in my direction, over and over again, and I was wondering if the other people were OK.

After hours at the hospital getting x-rays, pills, more pills, more x-rays, I was given everything I needed for my neck---the neck brace was so nerve racking---I was driven home by my Uncle Kenny after my family had come and gone.

Now, just imagine me not being able to work for 13 days!

I am a busy-body and it was driving me crazy to just sit there. But, I read my Bible a lot, hung around on Facebook---and thanked God for being alive.

The other driver, I learned, was an 18 year-old student. Her little brother, 14, was in the passenger seat. I was happy to hear they were doing well--both received head injuries.

Sitting home one day, God began talking to me.

"I am not ready for you yet. I still have work for you to do and people for you to help."

People always ask me why I'm always happy or seem to always think positive.

"I'm alive," I say.

God has saved me over and over again. I believe I'm a walking miracle. I believe God was my co-pilot the day of my wreck.

"You were lucky you were driving that SUV," people say when I tell them about the accident.

"I'm not lucky," I said. "God saved me, not my car."

Chapter 40

I Hope You dance

I often reflect on my life in amazement about how it has turned out---thinking I would never reach 40 or that I would never live a fulfilling life because of the bad choices I made.

The first half of my life was tainted by traumatic experiences and bad decisions. I lived through childhood molestation, a cheating father, the separation of my parents. I witnessed a murder, nursed a youthful broken heart and got involved with the wrong crowd at school.

Then I was drawn into criminal activities which included hustling, cheating. Finally, I was betrayed by a good friend, considered checking out, went to jail, had a scare with the HIV test--- the list goes on and on.

Even with the bad experiences, I still have many memorable moments in life: discovering and supporting the Dallas Cowboys--even after 30 years, making good friends, learning about God, laughing about catching a wild possum, falling in love, purchasing my very first car at a young age, living a high life, enjoying the attention of the ladies, becoming a father, turning over a new leaf.

I was able to get my priorities of my life right: getting married, owning my own business--over 15 years and still going strong, rebuilding my relationship with my father after 21 years--slowly but making good progress, was a start.

Although I veered off the track a few times, I never gave up on pursuing the path to righteousness. I neglected God for a while, but I did not give up on him. He, in turn, never gave up on me.

God loves me unconditionally and has watched over me through the good and bad times. God has never betrayed me or left me empty--even when life dealt me brutal circumstances.

I tried blaming God for all the bad and traumatic experiences, especially when I felt I was being treated unfairly. Little did I know, He was testing me--to prepare me for my journey into the next chapters of my life.

At one point in life I felt I was invincible. Then, my eyes were opened and I realized I am a mortal like everyone else. I realized I felt the same pains as everyone else. I realized I was not above anyone.

Even so, I battled with my inner self. I drove away everyone that loves me. I guarded myself from the world. I was heading down a path that led to many forks.

Those paths led to other destinations. Would I settle for the path least traveled? There were paths of no return, paths where the bridges were out. Would I take the path of my past?

Or would I take the Path of Righteousness?

After a deep and meaningful moment with God, I found new strength to continue on. I reconsidered my options.

Life is about taking chances. With the right choice, you can find enlightenment, you can find happiness.

It is called the Road to Redemption.

I learned not to take life for granted---especially when I was given a second chance to get it right. I did not sit around, wasting my life. I made the most of life's precious moments, by working to achieving the goals in my life.

One major accomplishment has been to reach out to those in need and make them understand how I got here. I was able to make others see through the eyes of a man who has traveled the long lonely road.

Another major achievement is to inspire others to step out on faith as I have. God has spoken to me and instilled in me the ability to motivate all who are around me and beyond. I want to let everyone know that in God is our salvation.

This is the purpose of this book.

In April 2009, even as I was fulfilling my life goals, I had a near death experience. Since then, I have tried to live life to the fullest. I have tried living every day as if it were my last.

I choose to live.

I choose to dance.

With these last words, I say, "I hope you dance."

I hope you dance. (One of my favorite songs)

Father's Day Speech

Of all the rocks upon which we build our lives, we are reminded today that family is the most important. And we are called to recognize and honor how critical every father is to that foundation. They are teachers and coaches. They are mentors and role models. They are examples of success and the men who constantly push us toward it.

But if we are honest with ourselves, we'll admit that what too many fathers also are is missing — missing from too many lives and too many homes. They have abandoned their responsibilities, acting like boys instead of men. And the foundations of our families are weaker because of it.

You and I know how true this is in the African-American community. We know that more than half of all black children live in single-parent households, a number that has doubled — doubled — since we were children. We know the statistics — that children who grow up without a father are five times more likely to live in poverty and commit crime; nine times more likely to drop out of schools and 20 times more likely to end up in prison. They are more likely to have behavioral problems, or run away from home or become teenage parents themselves. And the foundations of our community are weaker because of it.

How many times in the last year has this city lost a child at the hands of another child? How many times have our hearts stopped in the middle of the night with the sound of a gunshot or a siren? How many teenagers have we seen hanging around on street corners when they should be sitting in a classroom? How many are sitting in prison when they should be working, or at least looking for a job? How many in this generation are we willing to lose to poverty or violence or addiction? How many?

The second thing we need to do as fathers is pass along the value of empathy to our children. Not sympathy, but empathy — the ability to stand in somebody else's shoes; to look at the world through their eyes. Sometimes it's so easy to get caught up in "us," that we forget about our obligations to one another. There's a culture in our society that says remembering these obligations is somehow soft — that we can't show weakness, and so therefore we can't show kindness.

But our young boys and girls see that. They see when you are ignoring or mistreating your wife. They see when you are inconsiderate at home; or when you are distant; or when you are thinking only of yourself. And so it's no surprise when we see that behavior in our schools or on our streets. That's why we pass on the values of empathy and kindness to our children by living them. We need to show our kids that you're not strong by putting other people down — you're strong by lifting them up. That's our responsibility as fathers

And that is why the final lesson we must learn as fathers is also the greatest gift we can pass on to our children — and that is the gift of hope.

I'm not talking about an idle hope that's little more than blind optimism or willful ignorance of the problems we face. I'm talking about hope as that spirit inside us that insists, despite all evidence to the contrary, that something better is waiting for us if we're willing to work for it and fight for it. If we are willing to believe.

That is our ultimate responsibility as fathers and parents. We try. We hope. We do what we can to build our house upon the sturdiest rock. And when the winds come, and the rains fall, and they beat upon that house, we keep faith that our Father will be there to guide us, and watch over us, and protect us, and lead His children through the darkest of storms into light of a better day. That is my prayer for all of us on this Father's Day, and that is my hope for this country in the years ahead. May God bless you and your children. Thank you.

Father's Day speech excerpts(2008)

----President Barack Obama

As a man, I've been representative of the values I hold dear. And the values I hold dear are carryovers from the lives of my parents.

So I had to be careful. I recognized the responsibility that, whether I liked it or not, I had to accept whatever the obligation was. That was to behave in a manner, to carry myself in such a professional way, as if there ever is a reflection, it's a positive one.

I decided in my life that I would do nothing that did not reflect positively on my father's life.

A good deed here, a good deed there, a good thought here, a good comment there, all added up to my career in one way or another.

I'll always be chasing you... Glory.

----Quotes by Sidney Poitier

Family acknowledgements:

I have seen all the work you put in writing this book. I'm so proud of you, and really looking forward to all the success the book will bring. I know its going to inspire someone out there. Congratulations and I wish you all the best.

---Love Gloria.

Congratulations on your book pops! I'm sure it will touch others as it has touched me ---Mercedes Barnett (19)

I love you daddy!---Sydney (4 years old)

Congratulation on your book dad! I bet your book will be a success, because they will enjoy your wonderful book. You will inspire the world!

---Love Madison (10 years old)

Congratulations on your book daddy. I know you have worked very hard on it, and I know you are going to do well. Good luck and can't wait till it comes out.

I love you---Ashley (15 years old)

Colleagues

I witnessed all the hard work behind the scenes--the dedication and passion incorporated to produce, what will be a huge successful book. Congratulations on the completion of your journey written in an Autobiography. I visualized that I had traveled back in time and was standing beside you. With each chapter, I felt your sorrow, your mistakes, your laughter, your joy--your triumph. Thank you for letting me be a part of your truly amazing journey.

-- Kim

President

2WorldsEntertainment Inc.

I want you to feel real special cause I usually don't read anything but the "Bible" and the Obituary! --Acquanita Harris

VP of Public Relations

2WorldsEntertainment Inc

A best seller!!!!! --Maurice Jackson
VP of Marketing

2WorldsEntertainment Inc

It has been a pleasure to work with you, Spencer. By God's grace, this book will be the beginning of something new for the many who read it.

- --Candy Green Gustavson

Chief Editor

2WorldsEntertainment Inc.

Additional Acknowledgement

To all my cousins: Wanda and Shelia Jackson and the kids--Love you guys--Red, Mike-Mike, Pumpkin, Betty Jean, Tony, Denise, Scooter (RIP), Joann, Lamont, Marquis, Lil Man, Mario, Pookie, Weedie, Corey, Patrice and family, and all my other little cousins.

To all the people: who helped me with this book—I couldn't have finished without…printers, cover designers, editors—Joanna and Marcus, Kim Luong, Candy Green Gustavson--Thank you for everything, for all your dedication and involvement in achieving the completion of my book. All your hard efforts have made a big difference which has greatly impacted the outcome.

To my Uncle Oscar Agurs: I have always looked up to you and tried to the best of my ability to be like you since I was a little boy. Thank you for being the fantastic person that you are and being the guide for me as I was growing up.

To Sidney Poitier: I lived my life looking at you as my hero and role model. I didn't always make the best decisions or do the right thing, but I always tried to keep you in my plans, right down to tucking my shirt in. You shaped my life. I try to carry myself as you would, and I even named my daughter after you-

-Sydney M. Barnett--Thanks for your contribution to the world and my life.

To the author Devondia R. Roseborough:
It was not until you suggested, I put it on paper that I realized the impact my story would have on someone's life--or that I may help save someone's son, helping him see through the eyes of a man who has experienced the journey. I am so proud of you and your achievements.

I sit back and watch you dedicate yourself to sending the messages to everyone in Charlotte--and around the world. I wonder in awe. I am amazed at the persistence you display in caring for the youth of today. I have made a promise to give back to the community and look at you for inspiration on how to achieve my goals and serve my purpose within the community.

Your Raseberrirose Foundation is highly respected in the community and you are performing a great duty in changing the outcome of many lives at risk. I thank you once again. Keep up your great effort in what God has instilled in you. Be blessed. I am blessed and honored to have known you.

To some of my neighborhood friends: Big 50, Dirty Red--Trooper, D. Mills, Anthony Scott, Derrick Parker, Cameron Mitchell, Cameron Stafford, Papo, Lavonna Bynum--you the best, Lorna, Tracy Davis, Bug, Rita Miller, Thaliana, Tony, Tony Boys, The Simmons, Jimmy C--my uncle, Shona Birtha, Monkey--love ya, Big Cat, Pookie, Candy Baker, Barbara, Angela Rashed--so proud of you, Acquanita-thanks for the love.

More thank you's to: Mike Pulley for all you've done for me--it's never forgotten, the Big Homie, Marcus Massey: Keep pushing, bro., Tom Tom--no party like a Tom-Tom party, Lester--you doing big things, Derrick and Gwen Holley--love you guys, Ivory Stanback--for life. Special thanks to my sweetheart, Lisa Vance--all way back to Tyron Hills, James Vance, Makeeba, Beverly Davis--Thank you for 22 years of friendship, Tonya Key--Thank you for being a great mother and friend, Gironda Massey--always easy, Amanda Dykes, Ronette Winston, Tonya Featherstone—shortie, Marion Barnett—Bippy--we were young when we first started out, but we both matured into great adults. Thank you for all the support over the years: Betty, Money, Shan, Sister (RIP) Ovular and Eric.

To my school mates: Cedric, Chris, Tawanta, Paige, Priscilla and Russell, Nina McNair--my buddy, Carla, Allen, Anthony Tillman, Beverly Moore, Charlene A, Charlene M, Charlotte, Chenelle--Tempo, Chris F, Chris G Crystal--Steelers, Dana, Daniel Krider, the Grier Twins, Darrell Perry, Dawn, Edie, Eric, Felise, Gironda--Birdie, Javonne, Jaye Delai, Joy, K-Dre, Kim, Kristi Burris, Lance, Lemuel Hall--What up, boy?, Lysandra, Marie, Mary Fallie, Melanie, Michael

Pickett, Nicole Sloan--too short, Nina Mcvay--stop fighting, Octavius, Pervis, Petina, Patrica and Betty Mackin, Ramona--party girl, Reggie Grier, Sam Givens, Shante, Sherresa Falls, Spencer Clark--spud, Sybil, Tamara Thompson--Sadie's, Chapman Girls--Ladies, Teresa J, Lee, Tiffany Saunders, Toni Springs, Tony Maxwell, All the Tonya's, Vickie Hall, Wanda, James Moore, Pervis Thomas

To all my clients: Thank you for the chance to make your life easy. To No Limit Larry and Morning Madhouse for keeping us laughing and informed, Mrs. Jones--you are one of the personalities that has come into my life--even when I was full of stubbornness, you were always by my side supporting me--I love you.

Special thanks to: Terry, Adam, Rob Base, Tammy, Nessie, Lump, Prince, Mrs. Sister, Pig, Tameka, Puffy, Larry Davis--Thank you for being in my Life: Little brother Shawn, Jatton, The Jeters, Tiny Tillman, Tonya Tillman, Shawn Benton, Marcus Belk, Brian Oxen (RIP), Diana Crawford, Little Linda, My champ and neighbor-- Kevin Seabrooks, Nyree Kerr, Richard Kerr, Jennifer Hardee, Ronda--from Idlewild, Starann, Dee Dee, Jean, Charles Jones.

To all of the people...who prayed for me in tough times, the churches I visited over the years who keep my faith strong when I am weak.

Born on 3/25/1969 in Charlotte North Carolina, Spencer Barnett is a loving husband and a devoted father. Graduated from Garinger high in 1987--attend CPCC

He is the CEO and founder of his brand new company "2WorldsEntertainment incorporated" (promoting books, book signings, book events, tours, charity events etc). He is also the proud owner of "Spencer L Barnett Total Maintenance Services Inc" since 1995 to present.

Sydney Poitier and Barrack Obama are two of his greatest inspirations, motivating him to accomplish his goals in life--even naming one of his daughters "Sydney"

He was brought up as a Christian, who is blessed that God has chosen him to motivate others to take a chance to step out on faith---as he has.

He spends his free time volunteering in the community and doing charity walks, donating time and money to various foundations.

Information page

For Speaking Engagements and Book Signings contact:

Author Spencer l Barnett

2WorldsEntertainment inc.

P.O. Box 42708

Charlotte, nc. 28215

Email:a2worldsentertainment@yahoo.com

www.2WorldsEntertainment.vpweb.com

www.lulu.com/spencerbarnett

Carey Digsby-Darrell Perry

www.urbantymes.com

Dana Adair-Sidberry

motivationmktg@gmail.com

crgreen4editing@gmail.com

Praiz Bible and Books

5740 North Tryon Street

Charlotte,nc. 28213

www.ingramcontent.com/pod-product-compliance
Lightning Source LLC
Chambersburg PA
CBHW021048090426
42738CB00006B/236

* 9 7 8 0 6 1 5 3 2 5 0 6 4 *